ALL
CLEAR!

ADMIT ONE ★ ★ **A Practical Guide for First Time Leaders and the people who support them** ★ ★ ADMIT ONE

BY
MATT HELLER

the Peppertree Press
Sarasota, Florida

ISBN: 978-1-61493-551-3

Library of Congress Number: 2017914885

Printed October 2017

DEDICATION

*To my wife, Linda— for making me laugh
everyday and inspiring me to be
the best version of myself.*

*To my parents, Bud and Barb Heller—
for instilling in me at a young age that
I could do whatever I set my mind to.*

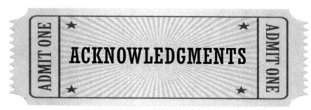

ACKNOWLEDGMENTS

A huge tip-of-the-hat to:

Jana Evanger, Elizabeth Nemeth, Matt Eckert, and Robbie Shofner for your invaluable feedback and guidance regarding the content and technical aspects of this book.

Vincent M. Giordano for once again bringing my vision of a cover to life.

Santa Cruz Beach Boardwalk for allowing me to use their historic carousel as a backdrop for the cover.

All leaders, colleagues, and friends who have contributed to this book, either through direct input or by the example you have set for others.

Julie Ann James and Teri Franco from The Peppertree Press for their continued support of independent authors.

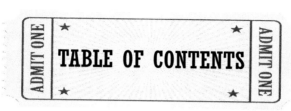

TABLE OF CONTENTS

S.M.A.R.T.E.R.   136
building bridges   149

PART III – Arms Up!
Management Tools For Developing New Leaders

10·18·2020

FOREWORD

Probably before I truly knew what it meant to be a leader, I was in a leadership role with the responsibility of training and developing other leaders. This wasn't an uncommon occurrence in the amusement park industry—young people with limited leadership experience were often (and still are) tapped to take on a leadership role—sometimes based more on availability than leadership acumen.

Of course I didn't know it at the time, but I probably wasn't as ready as I thought I was.

And that's the challenge with moving up into a leadership role. Often we think we are ready, or someone else does, and we find ourselves making decisions and taking actions on behalf of or for the benefit of others. Sometimes we're successful, other times we crash and burn.

As I began gathering information for a book about transitioning to a leadership role, I knew that I had to tell the story of Mark Pappas, someone I promoted to a supervisor position early in my role as a leader charged with developing other leaders.

Mark showed up on his first day as a supervisor wearing the traditional white shirt and tie. His khakis were pressed and his shoes sparkled. His radio crackled to life and the larger set of keys clanged as he walked out to his section. Later in the day, as I walked around to check on Mark and the rest of the staff, Mark asked me a question that quite frankly, I was not prepared for. He asked me, "Now, when someone calls me on the radio, who do I call?"

Dumbfounded, I said, "You. You call you. You are the supervisor. They are calling you to fix something or respond." The realization that the buck stopped with him gradually washed over his face. He slowly nodded his head. It was just sinking in.

Looking back, this situation now throws up a number of red flags, both for Mark and me. Mark may not have been ready for this promotion, nor did he have a clear idea of what he was supposed to do. Most notably, he didn't seem equipped for the weight of his new responsibilities.

For me, I clearly didn't prepare him well enough before he showed up for his first day of supervising. Maybe I even made the wrong decision in promoting him. Either way, the transition for Mark, from peer to leader, was not a smooth one.

That story inspired me to write this book for both the person going through this transformation, as well as the leader who is supposed to be guiding that person through it.

To that end, this book contains tools, resources, and information for people like Mark and the management teams charged with selecting, training and developing new leaders. While you can skip around to the parts you feel are most beneficial to you, I do encourage you to read the book in its entirety to get the full picture of what this transition is really all about.

A note about the title of the book: *ALL CLEAR* is the signal given by a ride operator when a ride is ready to dispatch. Depending on the safety protocol, it's often combined with a "thumbs up" from the other operators. This book is intended to prepare leaders to give the ALL CLEAR before taking on their new roles.

In the Station

Practical Information about
the Transition to a Leadership Role

Chapter 1
Suddenly Supervisor

There you are, minding your own business, when an employee comes up to you and wants you to solve a problem. And then another, and another. Then a guest, and another employee, and the phone rings, and you get a text, an email, and then another employee approaches you—oh, and there was that thing your boss wanted you to do ...

Learning to be a great leader takes time. And there is more to it than barking orders and doing the schedule. Leadership is about influence, vision, compassion, communication, drive, listening, initiative, awareness, service, and a genuine desire to make things better for others.

And, yes, I said "learning" to be a leader. There is much ado in HR and leadership circles about whether leaders are born or made. Here's my take.

On the one hand, there are people who, through their upbringing, learned experiences, nurturing, and personality appear to be natural leaders. You know the ones ... they are the people who get followed regardless of their title or official position. They are in schools, communities, and organizations all over the world, and sometimes even they don't know what they are doing to get others to follow them. They just do what they do and are labeled "born leaders."

Then there are the folks who show some of the promise of natural or born leaders, but don't possess all of the knowledge, skills, or abilities to consistently have a positive influence on others. They have the desire to get better at the craft of leadership, and just need some guidance and support to make the leap. These are the people firmly planted in the idea that leaders can be made.

I firmly believe that both scenarios are possible, and having a debate about whether it's "either/or" is fruitless. To do so discounts qualified candidates on both sides of the spectrum. With the NEED for quality leaders that we have today, that's not a prudent proposition.

But then there is a third group. You may know, or be, someone who falls into this category. These are the people who are promoted, because they are good at what they do—not because they are good leaders. One such example was Patrick Wymore.

Patrick was a ride operator in the Kiddieland section of the park where I worked early in my career, and he was a service superstar. He was incredible with the kids and parents, and every other operator in the area loved him. He was truly the poster child for what we wanted in an employee, especially one working around children.

So as the next season rolled around, we were looking for a Lead for Kiddieland and Patrick's name popped up early in the discussions. Here is what we knew about him:

- ▶ *He was well-liked*
- ▶ *He knew the operation of the area*
- ▶ *He was great with guests*
- ▶ *He was dependable*
- ▶ *He had great availability*

If you have ever considered the staffing needs of an attraction, you know that last one is key. And that may have weighed into the decision to promote him a little too heavily.

But we also knew he was well liked and was great with guests—that's got to account for something, too—right? What we didn't take into consideration was whether or not he WANTED to move up into a leadership role. Did he want the added responsibility? Could he handle it? Had he actually shown us that he could be a leader like we needed him to be?

Looking back, the answer was a resounding 'no'. Patrick showed us who he was, a great people person with a heart for service. Sometimes that translates to quality leadership, but unfortunately this time it did not. It turned into frustration, stress, drama, and a lot of head-scratching about where we went wrong. In our view back in the day, Patrick seemed like the perfect candidate. But he wasn't.

What Patrick didn't possess (and at the time we didn't know how to develop) were the tools to lead people— not just be their friend. That was probably a distinction that we (as the leadership team) didn't recognize well enough either. Maybe we had made that leap, but we weren't well versed in the finer points of the transition to be able to take someone with potential and turn them into a leader.

I will admit, I think I failed Patrick. I did not take fully into consideration his desire (or lack thereof) to be in a leadership role, nor did I do what I needed to do to make sure he had the tools to be successful.

In many ways, this book is for Patrick. Or maybe it's for a younger me, who wants to make up for what we put Patrick through. At the time, I didn't realize how important that transitional period was between being a peer and being in a leadership role. Jumping into that unprepared can have devastating consequences.

Here's the interesting thing. When I mentioned the topic of this book to my dad, he said, "We had that same problem 30 years ago in manufacturing. We would promote the person who was best on the line, or best at financial analysis, and make them a leader." He said that method rarely worked out.

Good to know we're not alone.

The transition that we will talk about in this book starts before someone steps out into his or her area as a new supervisor. It's about having a system to develop and evaluate talent, to make the right choices in which people you put into leadership roles, and supporting their journey once in the position.

ADMIT ONE ★ **AGAIN, TIME TO BUCKLE UP.** ★ ADMIT ONE

Chapter 2
Everyone Thinks They Can Lead

How many times have you heard a conversation like this in a break room, near a time clock or during a slow period of operation?

> *"Our supervisor doesn't know what he's doing! Can you believe he just did that? If I were in charge, things would be much different!"*

And so it begins ... the mindset that leadership is easier than it looks, and that it isn't a constant struggle to manage your tasks and relationships. Because we often don't have time to show people otherwise, it's entirely possible for frontline employees to get the wrong impression of what leaders do.

And that is one reason that new leaders fail—because they don't have a realistic idea of what they are stepping into. They aren't mentally prepared to deal with what's coming at them, so just like in other conflict-laden situations, their fight or flight instinct kicks in. And often it's not pretty.

Like Patrick they also fail, because they just aren't the right person for the job. Like any position we fill in an organization, we have to take the same, if not more, care to ensure the people leading our teams actually want to be there. Being a leader is NOT mandatory. We should not, for any reason, be putting someone in a leadership role if they don't have a desire to be there. In over 25 years of professional work experience, I have yet to see a "reluctant" leader work out for the best.

But here's the problem … you are trying to develop people and give them opportunities to grow, but the only "promotion" you can think of is to a leadership role. We'll cover more about how to deal with this in a later chapter, but for now we'll acknowledge that promoting someone to a leadership role because you don't know what else to do with them is probably not the best tactic.

Even if we get the right person in the right role, that does not guarantee leadership nirvana. The time it takes for a new leader to establish credibility and trust, to garner the respect of their teams, and to build relationships based on open communication is staggering. If you are reading this book as a seasoned and experienced leader, you know those can be lifelong pursuits—especially as the players on your staff change over time.

If you are reading this book as a newly promoted, or recently transplanted leader, or as someone who is training and developing a new generation of leaders, it's important to acknowledge that this process takes time. There are no substitutes for time, experience, and good ol' trial and error when developing leadership acumen.

Yes, even good leaders and those who should be and want to be there, will fail on occasion. The key is finding ways to NOT fail again in the future. People who want to be in leadership roles and have a desire to serve others in that capacity will naturally want to right their wrongs. They may not know how, but the desire will be there. One tell-tale sign of a reluctant leader is one who continues to make the same mistakes without really trying to correct them.

And if there is one thing that employees notice, it's when we make a mistake. What they also notice is when we make the same mistake repeatedly. Maybe this is where most employees start to get the idea that they can lead better than their leader.

What comes next is the deathblow to any leader. When an employee notices the trend of you making the same mistake over and over again, it leads to the idea that they can do it better, which in turn leads to a decline in trust and respect for the leader. Then it's over.

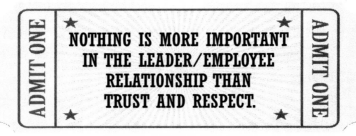

ADMIT ONE ★ NOTHING IS MORE IMPORTANT IN THE LEADER/EMPLOYEE RELATIONSHIP THAN TRUST AND RESPECT. ★ ADMIT ONE

Nothing. Nada. Zip!

Here's an interesting observation. When I talk with new leaders, they are often afraid of making a mistake, which is normal. They don't want to be seen as weak or that they don't know what they are doing. This can lead to even more mistakes because they are so uptight about doing something wrong! They think their leadership cred will plummet and they'll be a laughing stock.

But here is what I found to be true, and it's the opposite of what most people (especially new leaders) think.

When a leader makes a mistake, and they can admit it and learn from it, the trust and respect levels of their employees generally goes up, not down. This is because the leader has shown that they are human, which makes them more relatable, and that they are interested in getting better, just like they are asking their employees to do.

It's when leaders make a mistake, don't admit it, try to cover it up and continue making that same mistake that employees start to question their ability, integrity and whether or not they are a person they should really be following.

This is where Henry Ford's famous quote "Whether you think you can or you think you can't, you're right" actually DOES NOT apply in my opinion. Many people think they can lead. Many people think they can do better than others (especially when they don't have all the facts). Many people think leadership is easier than it looks.

It's not, and not everyone is cut out for it.

Chapter 3
A Leader's Mindset

To me, we can't talk about leadership, and especially the transition to a leadership role, without addressing the Leadership mindset. There is a real and vast difference between what goes on in the mind of a frontline employee and what happens in the gray matter of a true leader. It's like plants in a garden—of course they need sunlight and water to grow, but without the planting of the seed, none of the rest matters. The same is true of a leader's mindset … without the right thought processes and attitude, none of the rest matters.

Frontline Mindset

Let's go back to our days on the frontline to explore what this really means.

On the frontline, we were responsible (meaning we directly impacted) things like safety, guest service, cleanliness, sales, teamwork, capacity, and efficiency. When I say we directly impacted them, I mean this is what we did on a daily basis. We were the ones cleaning up the spills, we were the ones grouping people on the ride platform, we were the ones folding t-shirts, we were the ones cooking the food, we were the ones watching the water, we were the ones selling tickets ...

We had a direct connection with the guests, which means we had a direct connection to the product that the company was "selling." In the attractions industry, we often say that we sell fun, or that guests are paying for an experience, rather than a product or commodity. Whatever you want to call it, working the frontlines gave us unparalleled and unfiltered access to our end user and how they felt about our services.

And while each employee is different and approaches their work from a different set of circumstances, there is a mindset that is common to most people in those positions.

Since they are the "doers," their mindset is generally focused on the task that is directly in front of them. Whether it is their normal job duties or a special project, they are concentrating on getting that one thing done. Sure, their minds will wander to other things, but overall, they are probably most concerned with getting that task completed.

This is not a bad thing—in fact, it's necessary. Things don't get done unless someone does them! The spills don't get cleaned up and the tickets are not sold unless someone is there to make those things happen.

And almost no matter how long someone is in a frontline role, this mindset gets ingrained. It can be really tough to switch that mindset when stepping into a leadership role. Part of the reason for this is comfort. It's comfortable to stay in the role (and mindset) that we already know. How many leaders do you know who seem to fumble around with what to do as a leader, yet seem ultimately more comfortable when they can slip back into a frontline role? The truth is that new leaders often don't actually know what to do with themselves when they get into their first leadership position.

Someone else is cleaning up the spills and folding the t-shirts. What do I do now?

I remember my Dad asking me what I did all day as a newly promoted section supervisor at an amusement park. I think I said something like, "I make sure everything runs smoothly." Looking back, that was definitely spoken by someone still firmly planted in the Frontline mindset.

Why? Because that statement is largely reactionary and it's focused on tasks. To "make sure things run smoothly" implies watching over an operation and addressing issues as they arise—in other words, a firefighter.

And early in my leadership career, when I felt this was my purpose, I found myself checking on those things a lot.

"Let me walk over here and see if everyone is doing their job. Yep. How about over here? Yep. Okay, I'll walk to the other end of the park. Yep, doing their job, too. Everything seems to be running smoothly. I must be doing my job."

I thought I was leading. I didn't realize that all I was really doing was watching Frontline people do the tasks I used to do. And since I used to do them, I knew if they were doing them correctly. I thought I was leading, but I was just overseeing.

And that's where the term and the practice of "supervision" come from. Picture a manufacturing plant with the big window overlooking the production floor. In the window stands a *supervisor* … a well-intentioned overseer of all that occurs in his or her kingdom. And they probably still have a Frontline mindset, too. They watch workers and deal with issues as they happen.

Unfortunately, this is not leading. In order to lead, leaders must look at things from a different perspective. Developing that mindset is not easy, especially when you don't know what it is or how to develop it.

Compounding that issue is the fact that many current and experienced leaders haven't really developed that mindset either, so they are ill-prepared to develop this mindset in others.

Fortunately, I had someone in my past who knew a little something about this.

One of my earliest lessons in the change in mindset came when I was a Group Leader at Canobie Lake Park, directly in charge of six attractions. Admittedly, it took a while for the lesson to fully stick, but with this incident, the seed had been planted.

I was sitting at a picnic table in my section, where I could see all the attractions that I oversaw and they could see me. I was busy doing my weekly schedule when my supervisor, Mike Carchia, came over and asked how the schedule was coming.

"Just about done," I said. "Probably another 10-15 minutes or so."

"Great", Mike said. "Let's take a walk, you can finish that later."

"No, really, Mike. I am just about done. Can we take the walk in 15 minutes?"

"This is more important—you can finish that later."

Begrudgingly, I packed up my papers (this is back when schedules were done with paper and pencil—not a computer program) and fell in step with Mike. We started walking my area and Mike immediately made his motivations known.

"Who is running the Pirate Ship?"

A little confused, I said, "Hassan."

"When did he get here and when was his last break?"

After I answered, he continued the inquiry.

"Who is in the tower of the Flume? When was the last

time the operators at the Timber Splash rotated? Who is coming in to do your afternoon breaks? Who goes home at six, and who is going to replace them?"

After the bevy of questions, it hit me. This was more important than the schedule. He was making sure that I knew what was going on with my employees' well-being, because if I don't take care of my employees, there won't be anyone to put on the schedule.

Thanks, Mike. Point well taken.

And the point was this … as a leader, I was no longer responsible for the tasks. Not directly anyway. Now I had a cast of characters whose sole purpose was to perform the tasks that had a direct impact on the guest experience. As Mike was showing me, I was now responsible for *them*.

And honestly, that was an entirely new proposition. I mean, I think I've always been pretty focused on people and how they are doing, but this little experiment took that mindset to the next level.

It was the Leadership mindset.

And with that, my Frontline mindset was slowly fading and a new way of thinking was creeping in.

Chapter 4
The Leadership Mindset Applied

I have a friend, Doug, who works in the medical field and he recently shared with me that a new manager had taken over his department. He was actually kind of happy, because his last manager was out of touch and wouldn't hold people accountable to the standards they were hired to uphold. Doug was hopeful that the new manager would infuse some fresh energy into the team and reverse all the damage the previous manager had done.

Unfortunately, at least in the first six months, the new manager had also taken a hands-off approach. As Doug described it, she did all of her work and communicating through team supervisors, email, or by writing messages on a whiteboard in a common area. He said that after six months of her being there, some of the 50 people within her charge had still not met her yet.

Seriously? After *six* months? I hope you think that is as outrageous as I do.

Think about the perceptions that likely formed in that first six months. I could tell without even talking to Doug that the people she had not met likely didn't have a high opinion of her. Then he dropped the bombshell.

Most of the people she hadn't met worked the overnight shift. So you mean to tell me that in six months, she couldn't adjust her schedule ONE TIME to meet the folks working that shift? I've never met her, and even I'm getting a little angry with her. Imagine being on that shift and never meeting your boss WHEN SHE WORKS IN THE SAME BUILDING!!

Unacceptable.

Okay. Deep breaths. We'll chalk this up to a lack of Leadership mindset.

Let's turn our attention to something more positive, shall we? Like when Bill Davis took over at Universal Orlando Resort as the president and COO. In the first days and weeks of his arrival on the Universal "campus," stories of him "popping up" all over the place were making the rounds. He would show up at a department meeting, a merchandise stock room, a third shift maintenance area … all so he could get a sense of what was truly going on with the operation. You would see him out in the park, talking with guests about their experiences. But it was one instance that shaped my perception of the man, and told me all I needed know about where his priorities were.

One day, I was walking by the front door to our wardrobe building. This was right across from the main security gate that 90% of our team members would use to access property on a daily basis. Many of those were frontline, costumed team members so they would walk directly from the security gate to the wardrobe building. At the end of their shift, the process would repeat in the opposite direction.

As I walked by the building, there was a team member standing in the doorway, looking like she was ready to go home. At that moment, Bill walked out of the building and onto the sidewalk. He looked around, noticed the team member, then introduced himself.

"Hi, I'm Bill. What's your name?"

"Denisha."

"Where do you work, Denisha?"

"Food carts."

"Great! Wondering if you can help me out? See this mat in front of the door? Can you please grab one end and I'll get the other so we can straighten it out? This is one of the first impressions our team members get when they walk onto property, and we want it to be a good one."

Denisha helped him, he thanked her, and went on his way.

To me, that showed his commitment to the team members and demonstrated his willingness to get them involved. That's what the mindset of a leader does ... establishes priorities which ultimately guide your behaviors.

Of course, if he didn't exercise the Leadership mindset, he could have handled this in a number of different ways.

► He could have kept walking, ignoring both the mat and the team member.

► He could have fixed the mat himself, never talking to the team member.

► He could have told the team member to fix it by herself.

► He could have waited until he got back to his office and called someone to take care of the crooked mat.

How many of us have experienced "leaders" who performed one of these alternate actions?

What kind of impression would Denisha and I have if he had done one of these instead of what he did?

So, the application of the Leadership mindset begins with knowing:

ADMIT ONE

YOUR PEOPLE COME FIRST.

ADMIT ONE

They should be your priority because they do, in fact, make things happen. It should be one of your first goals to learn something about each of your employees and what they do so you can effectively guide and support them. Could Bill have met and learned something about each of the 13,000 team members at Universal at the time? No, and I really don't think anyone expected him to. But he did make the effort to get to know quite a few, and that was making a positive impact around campus.

No matter how many people you have on your team, you owe it to them and yourself to get to know them, just as you will get to know yourself as a leader. And before you say, "Well, I worked side by side with them last season, so I know them," think again. You know them as a peer. You don't know them as a leader. More importantly, they don't know YOU as a leader.

This process of getting to know your employees is also about them getting to know you ... as a leader.

And that's what made the exercise that Mike Carchia put me through both scary and liberating. Scary because I had to change the way I thought and consequently what I did, and liberating, because it showed me that there was another way to succeed—it wasn't all on my shoulders.

It's well-documented that change is often met with fear and defensiveness, which leads to closed-mindedness, over-reactions, and less than logical deductions. While I fully appreciated Mike's training, I knew it was going to take some time to fully embrace what it meant. I hadn't been in a true leadership role for long, but still certain habits had developed. I believed things, developed an understanding of certain priorities and processes (and TASKS!), and now that was all being flipped upside down.

I now had to approach my role thinking of people first, tasks second.

Like I said, I think I already had a good mind for people, but I didn't know what it really took to lead them. I was overseeing them, like the supervisor in the manufacturing plant, but I wasn't leading.

So I had to *understand what leading really meant.* I started reading books, attending seminars, and examining the people around me. One of the books that really had an impact on me was called, *It's Okay to Ask 'Em to Work*[1] by Frank McNair. The book outlined some very simple leadership concepts that helped me turn the corner, and I am forever grateful for picking it up.

One of the concepts that became clear to me at the time was just how important and complicated the leader/employee relationship is. That's true in any industry, but add to that the fact that in the attractions world, our young leaders are often just one step removed from working very closely with people they consider friends. Close friends. Besties. BFFs.

From personal experience and discussions with industry colleagues, that's one of the biggest hurdles that young leaders have to overcome.

What we have to realize from the get-go is not just how important that relationship is, but how it's *changed* since getting a promotion. Some of the change comes from you, while some is on the shoulders of your employees.

Many new leaders say, "I'm the same person I was before I got promoted." You may think that, but your employees don't. In many cases, it will take a new leader quite a while to realize there is now a difference of opinion on this matter. Once you get promoted, you are no longer the person in the trenches, working the hours, dealing with guests ... your former peers no longer see you as one of *us.* You're one of *them!*

And there it is ... the worst fear of many people, now realized. You are being rejected by your friends, excluded by people you trust, and discounted because you wear a different uniform. Some people just can't handle that, and one tactic to deal with it is to try to maintain the same level of friendship after they've been promoted. They don't have the benefit of the knowledge that that approach hasn't worked for hundreds of years, but they are going to give it a go—better than losing their friends, right?

The other method is to channel their inner drill sergeant and command respect. Drop and give me 20, maggot!

Neither of these work, so what's the answer? One of the most often discussed, but hard to achieve concepts in leadership and in life:

Balance

We will dive more deeply into this concept in Chapter 9, but in this context, *Balance* is about knowing your employees well enough to know what makes them tick,

---

[1] Frank McNair, *It's Ok to Ask 'em to Work ... : And Other Essential Maxims for Smart Managers* (AMACOM Div American Mgmt Assn, 2000).

while also keeping enough distance to be objective and not be exposed to the kinds of shenanigans that lands young people in hot water. Back in the day, that was relatively easy. Once promoted, you had to limit the time you spent with your employees outside of work. That generally set the tone that you were no longer running in the same social circles. That can sting a little bit, especially when you hear your friends talking about what they did the night before and what a good time they had. But, if you are committed to being a leader, it's a critical step.

Of course in 2017, things are a little more complicated. We're all connected via social channels, and the prickle of severing those connections can be unpleasant.

Again, if you are committed to being an effective leader, it's a necessary step. The access you have to your employees, unfortunately, can put you in a very difficult position.

Let's say you are Bill's supervisor. Up until this season, you and Bill had been peers, working in the same food stand for a few seasons. Because of your friendship, you and Bill are connected on Facebook and Instagram. One day, Bill calls in sick and doesn't come to work. Later, when you are scrolling through Instagram, you notice a picture of Bill at the beach with some other friends on the day that he had called in sick to work.

As his supervisor, what do you do? You now have evidence that Bill lied to you and put the team in a

29

tough position because you were short-staffed that day. If he were sick and unable to come to work, that's one thing. But, Bill clearly wasn't sick.

Your company probably has some rule or policy about being honest or acting with integrity, and Bill could certainly be disciplined for his actions. However, because you found out about this on social media, it's easy for Bill to get very defensive and accuse you of spying on him. He might even try to appeal to your sense of loyalty as a friend so you'll go easy on him, which puts you in a tough spot as a leader and most certainly (if history is our guide) will put a strain on the relationship.

In order to save that frustration and maintain a balance of friendship and leadership, clear boundaries must be set immediately when you take a leadership role, so you are both prepared for what's about to happen.

And it's incumbent upon the person taking on the new responsibility to proactively address these types of issues before they spiral out of control. If you are looking for an easier way to handle this, or think things will just magically work out, you're wrong. It's that simple.

Boundaries to be set include:

▶ **Social media** - Have your own social media policy and explain it to those who are affected. Tell them you will be unfriending them, but it's not because you don't like them, it's to save both of you the aggravation. *LinkedIn* is generally for more professional relationships, so remaining connected there is usually acceptable.

▶ **Non-work contact** - It's okay to still hang out with people you are friends with outside of work, as long as you are not putting yourself in a compromising position. This would include anything that would jeopardize your relationship and ability to lead, such as sharing confidential information, discussing other employees, or badmouthing the company or other leaders.

▶ **At work conduct** - You have accepted the role of a leader, and with that comes certain responsibilities and expectations of behaviors. Let your friends know what those responsibilities and expectations are so they can help you achieve them, rather than hinder your progress. Also let them know that part of your job is to monitor, recognize, coach, discipline, and lead EVERYONE on the team, and that *no* special favors will be granted. You will not look the other way when they screw up, assign them the best jobs, or reassign certain people to work together. In other words, no preferential treatment, no favoritism.

Having these conversations up front does a couple of things:

▶ Lets your employees know where you stand so there is no confusion. Maybe it's human nature, but we like to push the envelope when we don't know where the edges of the envelope are. Be clear on the edges (and what will happen if they are crossed).

▶ Allows your "frienployee" to get behind you to help you succeed. You may be one of "them," but by bringing people into your circle and allowing them the chance to help, you've shown you trust them to do the right thing. This gives them something to think about, rather than spending their time sabotaging you because they don't know why you've changed.

▶ Sets the stage for future accountability. It's much easier for us to say, "Remember when we talked about X," when someone gets out of line, rather than to try to explain the rule or expectation in the heat of the moment or after the fact. That often comes across as though we are making things up as we go along.

And this accountability is for us, too. As the saying goes, "A promise spoken is a promise kept." Openly sharing our expectations with others makes them more real, more tangible, and if we have said what we are going to do, we know we'll look bad if we don't. It's a funny little motivation game we play with ourselves, but it seems to work!

Full disclosure on the previous section: I am 47 years old at the time of writing this chapter. I know full well that some people who are younger than I am are going to bristle at the concept of separating work from friends. In fact, you may have even taken the job because of, or had been recruited by, a friend in the first place. We all know this is a very social atmosphere we work in and, in fact, we emphasize that aspect when recruiting new employees.

I also fully recognize that in 2017, seemingly more than any other time in history, there is a much heavier focus on family, friends, and the relationships that make life exciting and fulfilling—and that can be at odds with someone's career path. When you make the choice to be a leader, you have to realize (and accept) that there are going to be changes to established relationships. It's a fact. There are no short cuts, no do overs, and no get out of jail free cards.

These changes don't have to be bad. Handled correctly, the relationships you have already established can become stronger if you approach the transition to your leadership role proactively—being mindful of all the landmines that await you at each and every turn. Handle the transition poorly and you risk damaging relationships, hurting the business, and frustrating yourself.

Whether 1990 or 2017, navigating the change in relationships can be difficult, especially if you don't embrace and establish the Leadership mindset. You are now responsible for *people*, and that is not a situation to be entered into lightly.

Chapter 4a
Before We Go Any Further ...

It's important to remember:

All this talk of Leadership mindset, changing relationships, and new social media realities is just too much for some people to take.

And that's okay.

While difficult, if you really don't want to be in a leadership role for any reason, don't be afraid to admit it. We've talked about the pitfalls of being the manager who puts someone into a leadership role before they are ready, but we also need to address what goes on from the new (or reluctant) leader's point of view.

If you are in a leadership role, but it's not working out, you will likely admit it to yourself before telling anyone else. Tell your staff? No way, you'll be a lame duck leader ... if that! Tell your boss? Not a chance! They trusted me to do this, I can't let them down.

But I would say it's more of the opposite. If you choose to stay in a leadership role that you don't belong in for longer than you should, you will let yourself, your team, AND your boss down.

When you say that a leadership position is not for you,

you're not admitting defeat, you're admitting that you recognize this is not a good fit for you. Just like working at a new company or taking another job within the same company—you don't know everything that is involved until you really get into that role. And it's much better for you to recognize that and move on in the early stages, than staying on too long, creating a frustrating environment for you and everyone around you, all while struggling with something you really don't want to be doing.

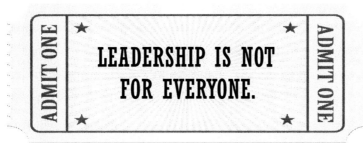

Thing is, a leadership role can be tempting. More money, better title, and respect! People will respect me if I am promoted! Really? How many leaders do you NOT respect? It's not the title or a different colored shirt that determines how much others respect you.

Taking on a leadership role can also be tempting because your managers want it to be that way. Remember Patrick? Quite honestly, I don't remember what his reservations were about taking the role—and clearly it didn't matter to us at the time. I (and the other managers) wanted him as a Lead, and by golly, we were going to make him a Lead.

Did I just say we were going to "make" him a Lead? Wow. I just realized, right now, as I am typing this page in the book, how badly I bungled the approach with Patrick. I probably tempted him with accounts of how cool it was to be a Lead, what was in it for him, and some of the wonderful things he was going to get to do in his new role. I guess we were persuasive because he took the position. If you have read Chapter 1, you know how that turned out.

If I may, let me try to possibly grasp what might have been going on in Patrick's mind. He was being courted for a leadership role his second year at the park. His managers were telling him how great he did last season, how wonderful it would be to use his talents to spread great guest service throughout his entire area ... all you have to do is wear this blue shirt, carry a set of keys, and answer when we call you on the radio.

Was he being courted, or coerced? Strong-armed? Bamboozled? Looking back, I feel like the slick salesman for the magic elixir show we had in the park that year. Saying whatever he needed to say to get the chump standing in front of him to buy whatever crazy potion he was selling. How do you say 'no' to the elixir salesman? You don't.

So could Patrick have said 'no' to us? Unlikely, unless he had a really strong conviction about not taking the role, he was clairvoyant enough to see the future, or if he knew from previous experience that this was not the right move for him.

To how many people do those conditions apply? In my experience, none. It's unfortunate that many of the people we are putting (or pushing) into these roles don't have the life experience to know whether or not it's the right move, nor do they have a crystal ball to predict how it's going to go. Even if they did, it would be rarer still for them to have the maturity and skill to eloquently tell their supervisor that they aren't interested.

Plus, how many of our young employees would jump at the chance to move into a leadership role—especially if we make it sound better than it is? In many ways, this isn't a fair fight.

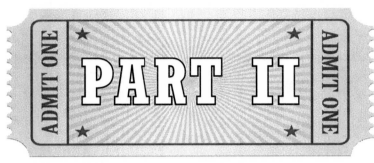

On the Lift Hill

Tools and Resources for Those Moving Up

You've identified that this leadership thing IS for you. You want the role and feel ready. You even feel your mindset starting to change. The slow metamorphosis from frontline employee to leader has begun. But like Mark Pappas, you have questions. Particularly, "What do I DO now?"

Since people are your new priority, it makes sense to start there. How do you lead, inspire, guide, and manage people?

Chapter 5

Go Forth and Lead—
Relationship Management

Embracing the Leadership mindset means looking at things differently. From the perspective of those you lead, you are no longer an "us." You're a "them."

Who is this "them" we're talking about? Them, or they, are your new peer group. They are the ones with whom you now share a title. They are the ones who do what you do, and some may have been doing it a lot longer than you have.

They are also the ones who can help you acclimate to your new surroundings and be successful, or they can pretend you don't exist. Here's the good news: it's largely up to you. When you take on a leadership role, it's a lot like starting a new school year. There are new faces and experiences, and you don't really know your place. Remember how fun that was?

You had the shy kids, popular kids, jocks, cheerleaders, band nerds (I was one of those), smart kids, and everyone else who defied an easy high school label.

I'm not going to go into a whole "Breakfast Club" thing

here, but suffice it to say that each of these groups had a different way to approach a new situation – just like leaders taking on a new role.

ablaze

How will you approach it? Will you come in guns a'blazing, or will you take time to get your bearings before making waves?

I just happen to have a story of two leaders who had different approaches to a "new leader" situation. One of them was me.

We had both worked at different parks for several years, and had worked our way up our respective ladders. Hitting what we felt was a bit of glass ceiling, we both sought employment with a larger, year-round facility to further our careers. That meant, for both of us, starting over as frontline employees, working our ways up the bigger ladder of this bigger company. We both saw it as taking a few steps back for the opportunity to be able to take many steps forward.

We also made these decisions completely separately. It wasn't until we both moved across the country to this new location that we met each other and realized the similarity of our paths. Not only that, but we both have names that begin with 'M'—imagine that.

So here we are, Mike (name changed) and I, both working in rides at this new park, trying to prove ourselves. And our approaches could not have been more different.

Mike decided that his best course of action to lead him up the ladder would be to share his experience with the current management team. Not a bad practice, since he did have a lot of experience, but it was the frequency and the tenacity with which he decided to share. Even before he could have possibly had a good handle on the current operation, Mike was vehemently opposing management decisions. He would often offer suggestions starting with, "This is how we did it at (previous park)."

It's not that Mike had bad suggestions or ideas, but he was essentially, and frequently, telling the current management team that they didn't know what they were doing and that he knew better. Some people took his input with a grain of salt, others just found him to be annoying.

If you know me at all, you can imagine that my approach was quite different. Probably because of my personality, I downplayed my previous experience. I would certainly tell people if they asked, but rarely would I blurt out that I had already had ten years of amusement park operations experience. That's just not me.

Plus, I was of the attitude that this new park, since it was part of a much larger company than I had come from, probably did some things better than my previous employer. I was excited to learn about how they did things, so I watched and listened.

I also tried to be the model employee ... provide great service, come in on time, be in uniform, get along with my co-workers—the whole enchilada. I loved what I was doing, so it wasn't really a stretch.

43

After a few weeks on the job, I was promoted to trainer. After two months, Team Lead. As the current leads and supervisors got to know me and my background, they started coming to me for advice and guidance.

It may seem as though I am advocating for the "observe first" method, and probably to a degree, I am. Not just because it worked for me, but because of the relationships it allowed me to build within the team. There is a downside here, and that is that at some point you do have to make a stand and let yourself be known. Even though my "trajectory" at that park was swift, that might not always be the case. You have to know when it's appropriate to stick your neck out and when it's not.

When you do finally break the employee/leader barrier, do so confidently. Don't be a jerk, but be respectfully assertive and put your ideas out there in a clear way. Some people will still see you as an employee, and may not be prepared for this type of behavior from you. Even the ones who are ready, and even expected it, may be taken aback when it happens. Don't misinterpret their surprise for rejection. They may just have to get used to the idea of you BEING a leader, then get used to your ideas.

What this shows is that the relationship has to be established in order for people to listen to you and to respect you.

And you will find that your success as a leader is greatly influenced by the relationships you are able to build. Think about your own work experience ... who were you more willing to go the extra mile for? The person you barely knew who was barking orders at you or the person with whom you shared some common bonds and genuinely cared about their well-being (and vice versa)?

The reason this chapter is called relationship management and not relationship building is that you can "build" relationships that don't work. You can say the wrong thing, do the wrong thing, or not say or not do the right thing, and you could jeopardize a working relationship. Especially as a leader, relationships do need to be monitored, nurtured, and yes, managed.

This is not to say that we need to take a data-driven, robotic approach to relationships—not at all. This just means that we have to be ever more conscience of our actions and how they may impact or influence someone else. Leaders are ALWAYS being watched and scrutinized, and an innocent comment or gesture can be taken out of context or in the wrong way. Is that unfair? Perhaps. But you signed up for this leadership deal and that just goes with the territory.

This is why potentially distancing yourself (via social media) is a good idea for new leaders. As we have already discussed, those lines between leader, friend, and employee are blurry enough without having Facebook, Twitter, Instagram, or SnapChat adding to the messiness.

As you develop new habits and things you will be doing with your time, consciously making time for all of your employees should be top on the priority list—and morning meetings don't count! You may have a captive audience for your download of information, but this is not the same as taking one-on-one time to get to know your team.

When I was an Operations Area Manager at Valleyfair, I made the ~~conscience~~ *conscious* decision to spend at least half of my shift out in the park, interacting in some way with my employees. Sometimes that time was spent chatting with the ticket takers at the turnstiles, walking the miniature golf course with the ranger, or discussing the daily sales at the Skycoaster. It was also important to visit the people in the isolated areas, like the toll booth in the parking lot. And unless you are delivering supplies, do not drive out there. If they are expected to walk back and forth, show them that you can do the same.

The object was to *balance* my time between people and areas, while also not getting in the way. There is nothing worse than someone trying to talk to you while you are trying to do your job—don't be that person. Pick a time where there is a lull in the operation or if it gets busy, jump in and help. There were many times when an unexpected rush would occur at the turnstiles, and all-of-a-sudden, I was stamping hands. Or the flights at Skycoaster got a little behind, so I helped flight suit guests to speed things up. Working alongside people is a great way to get to know them … don't shy away from that opportunity when it presents itself.

At the same time, this is where relationships have to be "managed." You are not a frontline employee anymore, so while it was great that you helped your employees get through the rush, you don't need to (and shouldn't) hang around there all day. The rush is done, you've spent some time, now move on. Not only do you need to go spend time with other employees, those employees you were just with need their freedom and independence, too. If you are hanging around too much, they will probably start to wonder what else you should be doing and why aren't you doing it? They could also feel like you are hovering or micromanaging. Not at all the impression you want to give.

When you are going over what you got done on a particular day, you should be evaluating your relationships with employees as much as the tasks that you completed. Ask yourself if you contributed to positive relationships? Is there anyone you should spend a little more time with? Did anyone say anything that you should follow up on? Who are the people you tend to gravitate toward that may be perceived as your favorites?

When I evaluate the relationships I tried to nurture and manage over

Evaluating Relationships

the years, there is one that I totally destroyed when I was at Valleyfair. Thing is, *because* of the relationship, I should have handled this situation differently. But I didn't.

47

One morning I was walking the park just before opening and a call came over the radio asking me to call into our operations base. I found a park phone at a nearby game and called in. I was told that we got an anonymous phone call about one of our go-kart operators, Jack Santos (name changed). The caller said that she knew that Jack had come to work drunk and that he had alcohol and drugs in his company-provided dorm room.

Knowing Jack like I did, I didn't think this could be true. Up until then, Jack had been a near model employee ... great with the guests and a fantastic team player. I just couldn't believe it.

But, these were serious allegations so I knew something had to be done right away. Jack was on the schedule for later that morning, so I figured I would meet him as soon as he got in to get his side of the story.

Looking back, I really wish I had done just that. Instead, my mind raced to all of the potential ramifications. Drugs? Alcohol? There could be legal issues, so I had better bring in some reinforcements. On the way to the go kart track, I stopped and called Security. I told my story to the Assistant Director of Security, Ron (name changed) who said, "You did the right thing. I'll be out as soon as Jack gets here and I'll take care of it."

I felt better having some backup, but that reassured feeling quickly vanished when Ron confronted Jack.

He didn't ask for Jack's side of the story like I wanted to do. Ron proceeded to accuse Jack of everything the caller claimed. Jack denied it, of course, but Ron wasn't having it. Ron insisted on going over to Jack's room to do an immediate search for the drugs and alcohol.

You can probably guess what they found. Nothing.

So what really happened? As it turned out, Jack had been dating a woman who used to work for the park, but he had broken up with her the night before. She wasn't happy about the breakup, so she had vowed to do something to get back at him. Since she knew the parks' policies, she knew exactly what to say to get Jack in trouble, or to at least raise some suspicions.

Here's where I destroyed the relationship. By not going with what I already knew about Jack, I didn't give him the chance to state his case and defend himself. Instead, I set him up as guilty without all the facts and allowed another member of management to bully and wrongly accuse him. To say that I lost Jack's trust is an understatement.

Some people I tell this story to say that I shouldn't beat myself up about it, because it was Ron's approach that turned everything sour. While his approach was horrible, ~~it was me~~ I was the one who brought Ron in without giving Jack the benefit of the doubt.

And that's why I had to take the blame. Not just to myself—that would have been too easy—but also to the team. They deserved to hear me acknowledge that I screwed up. They deserved to know that I realized what I had done and would not be making the same mistake again.

Talk about a tough pill to swallow for a leader—admitting you're wrong and accepting the blame for something like this? But that's the territory we inhabit as leaders. With great power comes the chance to mess things up royally. Accepting responsibility for our actions shows that we are human and make mistakes, but won't allow others to take the fall for our shortcomings.

After all of this, Jack just wasn't the same. He had a chip on his shoulder and a real disdain for management—and who could blame him? I tried to regain his trust, but never did. He quit two weeks after this incident.

Part of relationship management is knowing what kind of relationship you have and whether it's strong enough to deal with these types of issues head-on. I feel like Jack and I had that strong of a relationship, and judging by his reaction, he thought so, too.

Your new peers

Other relationships that you will need to develop and nurture are with your colleagues in other departments. You may have had some contact with managers from around the organization in the past, but you will now be thrust into "equal" status—at least on paper.

Some of those managers will welcome you with open arms, offering to help you get your bearings. Others, probably through no fault of your own, will expect you to be up to speed immediately, or at least treat you with little respect or patience. Why would that be? Probably because they already have a contentious relationship with people from your department, and you are merely an extension of them. In fact, you may have gotten a warning from the higher-ups in your department, "Watch out for Dwayne in Maintenance. He has his own way of doing things and doesn't listen to reason."

Great, let's stay away from Dwayne, then.

But that's not really an option, is it? Dwayne is the guy who inspects your rides. Dwayne is the guy you'll have to brainstorm with if things go wrong. Was it operator error/ negligence, or did Maintenance miss something? If your relationship with Dwayne is strained, guess how often he might admit a mistake?

The question becomes—how do you develop relationships with these new peers? At some point, you are going to need something from them or at least for them to listen to you. What's the fastest way to build that bridge?

The foundation of that bridge has to be respect. Showing respect for their time, talents, and other obligations will go a long way in building a solid foundation.

Cheryl (name changed) was the accounts payable clerk at Valleyfair when I was there. I ordered a lot of products for

Park Services, so Cheryl and I interacted on a pretty regular basis. Cheryl was a pretty no-nonsense kind of person, and she didn't take kindly to people who didn't know, or didn't care to know, the proper procedures. I was actually "warned" about her when I first started.

My first step in building this relationship was to decide that it was worth building. I didn't want to be on the wrong side of such an important part of my business, so I took it upon myself to figure out what it was going to take to make this successful. Since I was the new person coming in, I put none of the early responsibility for building this relationship on Cheryl. This was up to me.

The next step was to learn to do things according to established procedures. This showed Cheryl that I was invested and willing to take the time to do things right. As a by-product, this also showed that I respected Cheryl.

When I did make a mistake early on, I was quick to apologize. Not only because it was the right thing to do, but also because it opened the conversation so we could discuss it and I could get clarification. The last thing I wanted to do was make the same mistake twice!

Working with vendors and payment procedures, there were always quirks. Always one or two exceptions to the rules. When I had a question about one of those, or anything else, I would always ask Cheryl if she had time—before launching into my query. If she was busy, while that information was important to me, it could probably wait. Once she was free, we could discuss it and get it figured out. This showed respect for her time.

I think in the end what helped solidify this, or any, work relationship was the willingness to give before I asked for anything in return. I gave of my time and showed Cheryl respect, and that allowed Cheryl to get comfortable with this new guy who didn't know a purchase order from an invoice.

Just like with employees, don't be afraid to ask your peers for their opinions, especially if it's in reference to how your departments interact or how you can best support them. Again, you are not asking for anything in return. Yet.

All this nurturing has to lead somewhere, right? Like when you need a favor or another manager has a resource that will help your team. The way you ask for that favor is critical.

If you have heard the phrase: "You catch more flies with honey than you do with vinegar," this would be the time to think about what that means.

When you are nice to people, when you genuinely care (and also say please and thank you), others are much more likely to want to do things for you. On the other hand, if you stormed in demanding cooperation, guess what you won't get?

In Chapter 9, we will talk about certain types of employees and how they can upset the applecart. You could likely see some of the same behavioral types in your peers. Since peers are people too, the same strategies can be applied.

Bottom line, relationships are emotional endeavors, and sometimes your best judge about those relationships is your gut and how you feel. It's important that this discussion of relationship management not get too clinical. The important thing is to be aware. How are you spending your time? Who are you spending it with? Are you working toward positive relationships with all employees, peers and leaders?

Not all leadership issues are black and white, and this is one area where there's a lot of gray.

Chapter 6
Obi Wan Leadership

One of my all-time favorite movies is *Star Wars: Episode IV*; what many call the "original" or "classic" Star Wars movie. It's the one that introduced us to Luke Skywalker, Darth Vader, Princess Leia, Han Solo, and of course, Obi Wan "Ben" Kenobi.

There is a pivotal scene in the early stages of the movie, when Ben asks Luke to accompany him on a mission. Luke hesitates, saying he will be needed by the family and can't get involved.

A few moments later, Ben utters the line that has stuck with me since I first saw the movie in 1977.

"You must do what you feel is right, of course."

For Luke, it was choosing between staying uninvolved and following what he thought was his destiny. If you have seen the movie, you know what he chose.

New leaders face dilemmas and choices all the time, not knowing what do to or how to weigh the options. Sometimes, I think if we take a step back and think of Ben's statement, it will help us make our decision.

Most of us, somewhere along the way, developed a sense of right and wrong. I believe I got mine from my parents, because it's their voices I hear in my head when a conundrum confronts itself. It is this 'sense' that I think new leaders need to learn how to listen to a little more closely.

Our sense of right and wrong can be referred to as our moral compass. How do we stick to a direction we just *know* is right? How do we know what choices to make to stay on the right path? These are tough questions that don't have easy answers, but they do have answers.

Your moral compass kicks in when you are faced with a situation that just doesn't feel right. You know those situations—you struggle with making a decision, because you know there is something off … a little hinky … not quite copasetic.

Picture this … you are a new supervisor, and an employee asks you for a favor. Their friends are coming to the park and they want an extra-long break, so they can ride the new ride with them. Not only do you recognize this violates company policy, it's not fair to other employees who don't have the same privilege.

But the employee is making a strong case … they don't get to see their friend (from out of town) very often, it would be great public relations (a personal escort on the new ride), and it won't take that much away from the operation (they will do it at the end of the break cycle so others aren't effected). This employee may have a future as a litigator, and while their reasoning may be solid in their mind, you know there is a bigger picture to be considered. The bigger picture, again, is about the company policy and fairness to other employees.

But I'll be honest, it's easy to forget that in the face of such strong arguments. Couple that with your desire to appease and please your employees as a new supervisor, and your moral compass may fail you. You may decide, well, okay, just this once I'll let them do this ... what could it hurt?

It could hurt a lot! But we'll get to that in a moment. The question that should be going through your mind instead of "What could it hurt?" is "Is this the RIGHT thing to do?" I would guess that just by asking yourself if it's going to hurt, you already know the answer.

So what are the consequences of doing something like this? You may think that you've done this employee a solid and they will forever be your friend and be loyal. That might happen, but I wouldn't count on it. What is more likely is that they will see that they can manipulate you for their own gain. Now that you have given in to this, what else can they get away with? This is not evil or malicious on the part of the employee, it's human nature. We are constantly pushing the envelope to see how far we can go in a job, in relationships, in tasks, and projects. Why would this be any different?

And that's just with THAT employee. Fear not, word WILL get out about what you did. Even if that employee assured you they would not tell anyone, someone is going to see them ride the ride with their friends. Then the questions will start ... questions you won't want to have to answer.

"*Why did Charlie get to ride the ride with his friends while he was working?*"

"*Um, because he asked.*"

"*So, if I ask, can I do it, too?*"

"*No.*"

"*Why not?*"

"*Well, um, because that was a one-time thing. His friends were in from out of town and I decided to let him. It's not something we do every day.*"

"*So, if my friends from out of town came in, I could get a long break and ride rides with them?*"

"*Um, no.*"

"*But Charlie did it, and you let him.*"

"*Yeah, okay, I did. But you can't and that's that.*"

"*But why?*"

"*Because I said so, that's why.*"

Whoa ... did you see that coming? Is that really what you wanted to say? When you took your leadership role, did you vow to not act like some of the ineffective leaders you've had in the past? Don't look now, but ...

Let's look at where this came from. It came from veering away from your moral compass. Your internal dialog was telling you this wasn't the right thing, but that voice wasn't loud enough or strong enough to influence your decision. Yet.

What if you had said no to Charlie in the first place? Charlie would have been a little upset, but he probably knew that getting you to go along with that was a bit of a long shot. (He may have actually been a little surprised when you did agree!). Being a little disappointed, he may seek solace and support from his fellow employees.

"Can you believe that Kathy wouldn't let me take a long break and ride rides with my friend?" (It actually sounds kind of ridiculous when you say it out loud.)

Do you think Charlie will get much empathy from his peers? I could see the opposite … "Well, I hope she didn't let you do that? That wouldn't be fair."

So that technique backfired for Charlie, but it actually worked for you. The other employees reinforced your fairness and leadership skills. They know that you can't be manipulated and probably feel better about your overall ability to make a decision. Bang-zoom!

The end result: instead of Charlie thinking he can control you and the other employees thinking you are spineless and unfair, you have an employee who sees the error of his ways (reinforced by his peers) and the rest of the team who is defending your actions.

Kathy thought saying yes to Charlie's outlandish request would foster loyalty, but if we look back, saying no would have actually fostered more loyalty and trust.

And that is the difference between long-term and short-term thinking, which is what Ben was trying to get Luke to think about.

"You must do what you feel is right, of course."

Right for the long run. Right for the majority. Right for the situation. We'll talk more about long- and short-term thinking later in this chapter.

In this example, the word 'fair' was thrown around a lot. Were we being fair to Charlie or the other employees? By being fair to one, are we being unfair to others?

Your ability to be fair and impartial will go a long way in building trust and respect among your team. Unfortunately, some people are under the impression that treating everyone *fairly* means to treat everyone the *same*—it doesn't.

Being fair is about considering the circumstances. Does one person get more recognition than another? Are they a better performer? If so, then they deserve more recognition, and as long as everyone has the opportunity for recognition, a higher performer getting more praise is perfectly fair.

In fact, it wouldn't be fair if your top performers were treated the same as mediocre performers. They require different things, different coaching, and different ways to support. Applying a "same across the board" mentality will probably do more to demotivate your top performers than doing nothing at all. That's not fair, is it?

Thing is, being fair takes a lot of time and communication. You'll have to explain to those making claims of unfair treatment that just because you didn't treat them exactly like everyone else doesn't mean you treated them unfairly.

This comes in to play a lot with promotions. "Why did Ethan get promoted when I have been here longer? That's not fair!" What this person doesn't take into account is that during their time with the company, they have been a marginal performer at best. However, because their manager hasn't had the tough conversations with them about upping their game, they think they are the star of the show. Communicating the reality of the situation will help them see that Ethan was, in fact, the right choice.

Without considering the fair vs. same quagmire, many new leaders will make unthoughtful decisions that seem right for right now, but will likely come back to haunt them in the future.

And thinking about the long-term outcomes of our decisions is one the trademarks of an experienced leader. Our moral compass is honed, or at least we know what it sounds like and will trust its guidance.

As an emerging leader, do you know what your moral compass sounds like? Or feels like? It could be a feeling you get when you see something out of place, something in your gut that says, "That's not right." This could be how you pick political candidates or a leader to follow. How does your sense of right potentially differ from others? The fact that it does differ makes following yours very difficult at times. Other voices may be louder, their arguments compelling, r`jc‍‍Boundary

but something inside says to you, "That's not right."

What IS right in your mind? How is that communicated to you? As I said above it could be a voice or a feeling. The key is to know what that is for you, understand how to interpret it and then follow it. That takes trust.

How long does it take to trust your inner voice or moral compass? Has it steered you wrong, or has doubting it or ignoring it steered you wrong? I would say for my life, it's the latter. How many times have you said, "I KNEW I should have done that differently!" Your moral compass was trying to tell you something, but you didn't listen.

The situation with Jack and Ron was just that type of situation. My moral compass was pointing me in one direction, but I didn't follow it. I have since learned to recognize the "voice" of my compass and have also realized how important it is to listen to it.

For a new leader to trust your moral compass, you have to follow it once or twice to see where it leads. Much like your employees will need to trust you to see where you will lead them, you will need to give your moral compass a chance to prove itself. Remember Kathy? What if she had listened to that nagging feeling she had? What if the voice to NOT grant Charlie's request was a little louder and she actually trusted that voice? She wouldn't be kicking herself for creating a team that doesn't listen to her and has no loyalty. And oh, by the way … remember earlier in the book when we talked about employees who think they can lead better than you? This is another nail in that coffin.

Like many other aspects of leadership, *saying* you'll follow your moral compass is much tougher than actually *doing* it. You, and others, will put up roadblocks that will have to be overcome.

First, you will likely misinterpret your inner voice/moral compass when it's trying to tell you something. You don't know the signals, the context, or the manner in which it's trying to communicate with you. You might think it's just a nagging thought or some bad shellfish.

Next, even if you hear it, you'll doubt your moral compass until you have enough experience with it to trust it. It's a fact. It's also why SO many inexperienced leaders fail. They get off course, run aground, and think in the short-term and not in the long-term.

Lastly, you won't initially make the connection between what your inner voice wanted you to do and what you actually did—even if it was successful. You'll attribute that success to some other factor than your own intelligence and actions, and your poor little inner voice will be left out in the cold. Is that any way to treat someone who is trying to keep you on the right path?

Others will put up barricades as well ... starting with arguments like Charlie presented. Well-articulated and convincing arguments that may even diametrically oppose your own sense of what's right.

After you have made a decision, roadblocks come in

the form of those who question you about why you decided to go in that direction. It may have been the right decision in your mind, in the eyes of your boss, for the good of the company, etc. Yet, someone will still be dissatisfied with your judgment, if they see that it didn't line up with their sense of rightness. So, they question you. You defend your position in a respectful and articulate manner, and while you may not change their opinion (you RARELY will), you may at least show that you have solid reasons for doing what you did. Most people, when given a chance to be reasonable, respect that someone has an opinion and is willing to stand by it.

If all this talk about your moral compass and doing what's right got you thinking about the concept of integrity, you are definitely thinking like a leader. Integrity is something that every leader is judged on … it's your ability to do what's right (even when it's not easy), to follow through on commitments, and to say what you mean and mean what you say.

Dictionary.com defines integrity this way: adherence to moral and ethical principles, soundness of moral character, honesty.

Over the years I have also heard integrity defined as "doing the right thing even when it's not the easy thing." Often, we are called upon to tackle the difficult tasks and make unpopular decisions—actions that can certainly land you in the leadership doghouse with your staff. But that can't be a motivation to shy away from the tough stuff—that's your job.

The reason these decisions often lead to confusion and distrust is that we don't take the time to explain our actions. Remember that frontline employees don't know all of what's going on with you and your world, so they might not agree with something if they don't have all the facts. To the best of your ability, be transparent and forthcoming with the reasons behind your actions.

In my experience, people do not respect or trust those who are dishonest or operate in an unethical manner. It's easy to forgive someone if they make a mistake. That happens. But when they willingly disregard the rules or the well-being of others, that's a pill that's a little harder to swallow.

Like trust and respect, integrity isn't something you can order from Amazon or pick up at the grocery store. It's something you earn through your behaviors and convictions. And P.S., acting with integrity is the fastest way to build trust and respect.

Here are some examples of behaviors that show integrity:

- ► Follow all rules that are set for you and the ones you are expecting your team to follow

- ► Follow through on promises

- ► If you can't follow through on a commitment, let the person know why

- ► Own and admit mistakes

▶ Address sub-par performance in a timely manner (in yourself and others)

▶ Recognize outstanding behavior in a timely manner

▶ Hold all employees to the same standards

▶ Treat everyone fairly, with a high level of respect

▶ Communicate in a clear and respectful manner

▶ Do not gossip or spread rumors—stop them if you hear them

▶ Never place blame on others for something you did

▶ Keep confidential information confidential—do not betray someone's trust

▶ Deal with problems head-on—avoid trying to circumvent or using back channels

▶ Be an advocate for respectful communication and treatment and address unacceptable behavior immediately

▶ Provide facts—do not speculate without all of the information

▶ Be a team player

▶ Avoid getting dragged into company politics

▶ Speak well about your co-workers and company and if you have concrete concerns, address through proper channels

This is by no means an exhaustive list, but it should give you an indication of the types of things you should and shouldn't be doing.

As I reread this list, it reminded me of things that might appear in an employee handbook. Why? Because acting with integrity is an important part of any employee's job, not just the leadership team. Leaders will be under a more powerful microscope, but those standards really do apply to everyone. Or at least they should.

If you have ever worked for a bad boss, or one who displayed a lack of integrity, consider yourself lucky. You got to witness first-hand what NOT to do and what the impact will be on the team around you. I sincerely hope that is enough motivation to want to avoid those types of behaviors in your own leadership career.

We started this chapter talking about doing what's right, and just finished a section on integrity. Isn't that a lot of ink to say basically the same thing?

Yes. But here's the deal. Being honest, having integrity, doing what's right … these are the things that will trip you up most as a leader. You will be challenged. You will be lobbied. You will question your moral compass and your own convictions. But there is one reason that you can't cave. One concept that HAS to keep your behaviors above board.

Do you know what it is?

You're a role model. I don't care if you don't want to be a role model, or you don't consider yourself one. You don't get to choose this. Once you accept a leadership role, you also accept that people will be watching you and judging your every move. And I mean *every* move.

They will watch how you treat other employees; who gets the "good" schedule and who goes on break first. They will watch how you handle yourself in times of stress. They will evaluate your character when the rules are disobeyed. They will wait to see what you do when they feel they are deserving of recognition or when they have screwed up. They will see if you jump in and help when it's busy or if you hide in the office?

So yeah, they are watching. This is why acting with integrity, building trust, doing the right thing, being honest, and *accepting* the role of role model is critical. When you know people are watching, you tend to be more aware of what you are doing.

If you need just one more reason to do the right things, think about this. Picture yourself on the witness stand in a courtroom. A lawyer is asking you to defend some specific actions you took as a leader. Can you defend yourself? Can you justify what you did and convince a jury of your peers, beyond a reasonable doubt, that what you did was right and just?

If the lawyer brought up other witnesses to corroborate your story, would they? Are you confident that your actions were observed and judged by others as right and just? It's one thing for you to say it, even to believe it. It's quite another for someone else to back you up.

That's a pretty high standard to hold yourself to, but that's the job of a leader. You no longer get to wallow in anonymity. You are front and center, in the spotlight, and it's showtime.

Chapter 7
Are You Greek to You?

In the previous chapter, we talked about listening to your moral compass, acting with integrity, and knowing what's right. This brings us to one of the lifetime axioms taught by the scholars at Delphi (sanctuary in ancient Greece where scholars would consult on important decisions of the time).

It sounds so simple. *I know my name, where I'm from, and what I like on my pizza. I know myself pretty well!*

But do you? Do you really know what makes YOU tick? It's hard enough for leaders to ascertain what makes the people on their teams tick, let alone themselves. Do you know why you act the way you do around certain people or under particular circumstances? Why is it that you mix with some people like peanut butter and jelly, but others are more like oil and water? Is it about them, or is it about you?

How can you feel all-powerful one minute and helpless as an infant the next?

Truly knowing yourself is a life-long pursuit, and listening to and trusting your moral compass is a big part of understanding your evolution as a human being. And make no mistake, you are evolving.

Think about who you were ten years ago. Chances are you share some characteristics with that person, but I would also bet that there are a lot of things that are different. You are you, and you live with yourself every day, so it can be tough to see the changes that take place over time.

So how do you get to know who you are now, not the person you were ten years ago? I think the first way to gather information about who you are is to listen to others, and I mean really listen. It may be tough, it may be uncomfortable, but when someone gives you a glimpse into yourself, through feedback, coaching or even an off-handed comment, take it! Examine what others say versus what you think to be true, and understand that their impression of you is the result of what they've experienced and filtered through their lens. That's enough to close off even the most open minds, because we think that other people don't get us, because they don't know what we've been through. It's the oldest defense mechanism in the book. In fact, it probably even predates the book!

When we discount someone else's opinion because they are not like us, we risk losing out on some very valuable information that could help us grow and develop in a positive way. Listening only to ourselves, or being stuck in the mindset of the ten-year younger version of yourself, is no way to approach a leadership role, where it will be imperative for you to know who you are and what you bring to the table.

By comparison, listening to ourselves is easy. We usually like what we have to say and agreement comes without challenge. When others share what they think of us or our actions, conflicts can arise, feelings can be hurt, and relationships can be damaged. That fear can be crippling, and can easily stop us from being open to any of the feedback headed our way.

This is where you take a deep breath, open your ears, open your mind and let it all in. Let it wash over you like sunshine on a warm summer day. Resist the urge to judge the content of the message in that moment. Give yourself time to process and understand it. Like the sun delivering vitamin D, you know you probably need this.

Once the information has had time to ruminate, assess it against what you already know to be true about yourself, your moral compass, and your relationship with integrity. You can't give back vitamin D to the sun, but you can choose how to apply the information you have just been given.

To be able to take in information from others and processes it so you can improve means you are coachable, and that's an extremely important skill to possess. You don't know everything, nor do you know how to do everything. Others are going to have valuable insight to share, which may contradict what you currently know. But it could also be a better way to do something … faster, more efficient, more helpful to employees, etc. Whatever the case, you owe it to yourself to listen. You can choose to close them out and discount their input for some random reason, or you can choose to admit that what they are sharing is valuable and that you have something to learn.

In addition to listening to others, it's also important to take stock of your own behaviors. Are there times when your conduct baffles even you? Maybe when you lash out at someone for no good reason, or step up when you had no intention to? Conversely, do you hold back when you know you should act? Why do you do that?

Let's talk about lashing out … how many of us have taken our frustrations out at the wrong time and with the wrong person? Everyone's hand should be up. We've all done it. But where does that come from? What was the trigger that set you off? Was it the person, what they said or did, or did the situation remind you of something that you have yet to get closure on?

I will state right now for the record, I am neither a psychiatrist nor a psychologist. However, I can say with great certainty that when people do not get closure on issues, they tend to bring them up at really inopportune times. Closure is this great thing that allows people to move on, to let things go, and to focus on taking steps forward. Without it, issues tend to fester and people become bitter under the weight of all those unresolved problems.

That's why understanding where your reactions come from and then taking action to get closure on the root cause is an important step in knowing yourself as a leader. You don't just lead others—you are also leading yourself.

So you are going to listen to others and examine your own behaviors. Great! But you're not done.

If you take the view that any insight is good insight, then you will also want to gather as many experiences as possible when learning about who you are. You may be in your comfort zone, because that's where you are ... um ... comfortable, but it's really hard to get new perspectives if you are always sitting in the same seats.

It's like going to a football game, and you have season tickets on the 40-yard line. That's great—you have a consistent view of the field and you know a lot of the people in the seats around you who also have season tickets. Do you ever, just for fun, get a seat in the end zone, or on the other side of the field? You'll see the game from a different angle and interact with different people. That's the same as getting new experiences to widen your scope of who you are.

New experiences that can change your perspective include joining a community club, a sports league at work, taking a yoga class, or going back to school. You may (no, you will) encounter new people who will test your view of the world and yourself. As a leader, that experience is gold.

You may also look to the world of academia or professional development opportunities to expand your horizons and perspectives. Online courses, books, and personal assessments are all ways to get a more complete picture of who you are.

I am a firm believer that the more you know yourself, the better you can lead. That said, knowing yourself is not about taking an inventory of who you are now and if you like it, sticking with it. Times change, people change and circumstances change. If you don't change and evolve, you'll be trying to lead a modern team with outdated techniques.

Which brings up the inevitable discussion being had these days about the various generations in the workplace. Bosses and managers around the water cooler lament the fact that today's young employees lack the discipline and work ethic of their generation.

This has become so commonplace that recently I was talking with a business owner whose daughter was complaining about the lazy millennials. Her daughter is 24, and by the way, a millennial! She's complaining about her own generation!

If you look at the word *generation*, it's very close to general or generalization. When we make generalizing statements, we are judging the many based on the characteristics of a few. We do it to make sense of what we don't understand and to rationalize behavior that is different from ours. When we talk about generations with sweeping generalizations, we are doing the same thing. This has a crippling effect on a leaders' ability manage their workforce, because they are more focused on how people are different rather than what brings us together.

Are there differences in how PEOPLE (regardless of generation) view work, society, teams, family, relationships, and the world around them? Yes. Deep down though, we all want and need the same things. To love, to be loved, to feel secure, and have a purpose. How one person gets there might vary greatly from another, but that doesn't make either of those paths better or worse than the other.

What does this mean to you? For starters, get over the fact that your younger employees aren't like you were when you were young, or the fact that older employees don't seem to "get it." Spending energy on that won't help you solve the problems you have. Understand that as communication methods change, as outlooks change, as priorities change, YOU must change, too. If you look for the value that everyone brings, you will find it, no matter the age or experience level. You can't get stuck doing the same things you did ten years ago. You'll never get ahead by looking back.

Here is an example to illustrate this:

Let's say that ten years ago, you could staff your park, center, or facility with people willing to work all day. They committed to you full-time, and you were their only employer. Fast forward and now where you have people only willing to work ½ days, fewer days a week and their

Swiss-cheese schedule is filled in with other jobs, friends and familial commitments.

What do you do? The obvious answer is that you'll have to hire more people in part-time positions to cover all of your shifts.

"But I didn't have to do that before!" you whine as you stomp your feet.

Have you added anything new to your property in the last ten years? Does the same argument hold water?

"We never had that exhibit there before!"

"We never gave away that prize before!"

"We never offered that food item before!"

Are you getting the idea? A little ridiculous, isn't it? Deal with the new reality—don't waste your time complaining about what used to be.

Just like any problem, you figure it out. The answer might not come to you easily, but no one said that you wouldn't have to think or do something you had never done before. Remember Mark Pappas? You are the leader. Figure it out!

The same goes for leading those who might be older than you. So many people in our industry start off their leadership career when they are young, which is enough of a challenge, and certainly leading those who were recently your peers is no picnic. But then there is the predicament of leading those with many more years of life and work experience. How could you possibly lead them?

How do you lead anybody? Get to know them, learn their strengths, weaknesses and desires, figure out how to support them and encourage them to greatness. I realize, of course, that within those simple statements, there is a canyon full of variables.

For people who have more experience, their experience is a strength. How can you tap into the reservoir of knowledge and wisdom likely tucked away in their head? You could *ask* them. Seek out their opinion and show that you respect the time they have put in. Realize that THEY know they have the experience, but may not express it until asked.

That said, you also have to demonstrate that you are an authority and are in charge. Not in a mean and overbearing way, but in a confident, firm, fair and understanding way. With anyone, if you are too wishy-washy, can't make a decision, and seem to lack any urgency, people will either A) discount you as a leader or B) actively try to undermine your efforts to be a positive influence.

And that brings us to Paul (name changed). When I took over as the General Manager of a family entertainment center, Paul was working there as a floor manager. He was older than me (by at least 25 years), had been working in the center for decades, and was once in line to take over as GM. He had some health issues, which prevented him from working the kind of hours necessary for the GM, so he settled into a floor manager spot.

Thing is, Paul had the "chops" to be the GM. He had intimate knowledge of the operation, he knew the employees, guests, and community inside and out, and his dedication to the place was unparalleled.

When I first arrived, Paul was very helpful ... maybe too helpful. He was great at getting me up to speed, but he also shared a lot of ideas of how to improve the place. Paint that, move this here, get rid of that, buy this ... it was, quite frankly, an overwhelming barrage of suggestions. So, I did what any inexperienced GM would do ... I made a mistake.

I sat down with Paul and told him that I needed some time to get my feet wet and see the operation from my perspective before making any sweeping or drastic changes. That doesn't sound so bad, even now. But what I failed to do as part of this conversation was to truly acknowledge the treasure trove of ideas Paul was sharing. Instead, and this was certainly Paul's impression, I was shutting him down. I was saying that I didn't value all of the time he had put into the facility and I also wasn't putting much value in him or his ideas.

Paul wanted nothing more than to help me, and I refused.

The silence from Paul was deafening over the next few weeks. He still did his job, but there were no more ideas, suggestions, or what if we tried this or what if we tried that? After a while, I realized I kind of missed it.

At one point, I overheard Paul talking to someone about painting our pool hall. It was looking a little drab, so a fresh coat of paint would probably really spruce up the place.

I got with our maintenance guy and asked him to look at some color samples and to price out the materials. I talked it over with the team, so we could work the project around our business, acknowledged (to the team) that this was Paul's idea, and said that Paul should roll on the first bit of paint to start the transformation.

At the end of the day, the pool hall got painted, but much more was achieved. Originally, I had lost Paul's respect, because I didn't show that I valued his experience and expertise. I didn't acknowledge that while I held the title of GM, he still had the knowledge and passion to be a tremendous asset. By implementing one of his suggestions, I was able to show that I did value his contribution, and did respect his experience. Then, the ideas and suggestions started flowing again.

Unfortunately, no amount of "knowing myself" would have prevented this at the time. Now, of course, I know my tendency to want to explore on my own and make my own impressions, but I have to be aware of the ramifications of "shutting others down" without meaning to. Sorry about that, Paul!

And you will likely struggle with these same issues as well. Like we said earlier, you think you know you, but you don't know yourself as a leader.

Slow down. Breathe. It will be okay.

Chapter 8
It's Like Riding a Bike ...

In the previous chapter, we examined the axiom of "knowing thyself" in order to be a better human being and a better leader. As an extension of that, we'll now look at the other concept near and dear to the hearts of those scholarly Delphonians:

BALANCE

If I had a nickel for every time I talked to leaders about the need for balance, I would have A LOT of nickels.

Just the other day, I was challenged in a class about the possibility of providing too much recognition. A passionate and experienced business owner asked me, "Can't you thank people too much? If they do something outstanding, sure. But to just thank them for showing up, that's a little too much. It will start to lose its meaning."

On one level, I agree with him. If we have no meaning behind our recognition, there will be no meaning for our employees. If we just say thank you because we think we are supposed to, we risk sounding like insincere drones delivering unimportant information. However, if our thank you's are sincere, genuine, and based on actual achievements, I don't think you can ever OVER recognize ... IF you balance that with opportunities for improvement and development. And it's a delicate balance, to be sure.

Positive

If you were to look at positive versus negative feedback, weighed out like on the scales of justice, how does the scale usually tip? More toward discipline and corrective feedback, or positive, encouraging feedback? In my experience, for a variety of reasons, it generally tips toward discipline and correction. That's needed, don't get me wrong. But the other side is needed, too.

Negitive

If you are still picturing the scale, think about if there is an overabundance of one or the other ... one side is grossly outweighing the other. What's the impact?

If ALL you do is praise, employees won't see that they have anything to improve. This could potentially lead to an over inflated ego on one end of the spectrum, or sheer boredom on the other.

If ALL you do is discipline, employees will never see that they actually are doing something right. Apathy and a lack of effort or innovation could be the results here.

So that's why we balance our feedback and recognition. But that's not all we have to balance.

► We balance our time. We balance the amount of attention one employee gets versus another. Similarly, we also balance the needs of the group versus the needs and wants of the individual.

► We balance our resources... knowing that overcommitting in one area means leaving another area short-staffed or ill-prepared.

► We balance our temper and emotions. Being open, approachable and showing you are human will help you gain trust. Showing your truth as an unpredictable hothead will do just the opposite.

► We balance finances. Money in versus money going out.

► And we balance relationships ... our boss, peers, employees, family, and friends.

If you read through that and pictured a clown at a circus trying keep an unprecedented amount of plates spinning in the air, congratulations. You understand the concept of leadership ... I mean balance ... or was it leadership?

It's all connected. And your ability to balance all of these things, to keep all the plates spinning, will be your ultimate test as a leader. And like many leaders before you, you will fail at times.

Be ready for it. Be ready to fail and fail big. No book (not even this one), leadership course, mentor, or video can prevent you from failing. But that's not something to be afraid of or shy away from. Failing is your friend. Failing is how you learn.

You see, all this talk about balance can't happen without that pesky little word: judgment. You can't effectively develop your ability to balance all the factors of your life and job by playing it safe or staying on the sidelines. Judgment is earned by making a decision, sticking with it to see the outcome and determining whether or not that outcome was good or bad.

Good outcome? Do it again.
Bad outcome? Do it differently in the future!

Sometimes decisions are made based on a gut feeling—other times they are more data-driven. That's another thing you have to balance, too, and that takes years to develop the proper judgment to do so ... do you go with your gut or do you go with the data? At times, the data can only get you so far, and it's up to your experience (your gut) to take you the rest of the way.

The unfortunate catch-22 of being a young (or new) leader is that you can't get true experience (and therefore judgment) until you *are* in the position. Hypotheticals and case studies are important and have their place in developing an analytical mind. However, you won't know for sure how something will turn out until you do it. And that can be scary.

But what should be even scarier is not knowing—always second guessing your decisions, because you lack the confidence to stand up and say, YES, this is how we're doing this. That can be a paralyzing proposition for someone charged with leading others.

Have you noticed that some people seem to make decisions quickly, while you are still analyzing the situation? Or are you the one making quick decisions, waiting for others to catch up? Either way, if we go back to the concept of "knowing ourselves," we'll see that our decision-making process is as much about the facts and figures in front of us, as it is about our personality.

Your personality is what drives your behavior … it's who you are. It helps you decide which way your moral compass points and what you put in the right column versus the wrong column. It also determines if you are more of an analyzer or one who shoots-from-the-hip.

Those are not official terms, and they oversimplify the study of personalities and behavioral styles, but I use them to quickly illustrate two major methodologies to making a decision—understanding that there is also a lot of perception in both approaches.

If I am an analyzer, I perceive someone who makes quick decisions as reckless or careless. If I shoot-from-the-hip, I might view an analyzer as weak and incapable of leading. Neither is true, per se, but they are a true perception in someone's mind. Knowing ourselves is more than just about knowing who we are—it's also about knowing how we are perceived by others.

Remember when we talked about trust and respect and building relationships? It can all be washed away in an instant if incorrect perceptions are allowed to fester and ultimately define who you are in the minds of others. Each and every interaction with you is a chance for your team to make a judgment about who you are and what you stand for. They will look at you, and perceive you, with the lens of: "How is this person impacting me and my life?" Again, it's not selfish—it's human nature.

Any leader who has taken over a dysfunctional team will appreciate this next story. To me, it illustrates how balancing communication and the needs of the employee versus the needs of the company CAN be achieved.

It comes from my friend Dallas Hobbs, who you may remember from a story in *The Myth of Employee Burnout*.[2] Fast forward to Dallas leaving that job to take over another team that was a little dysfunctional.

I left my last position because the culture was changing in a direction I was not comfortable with. It was difficult to leave a team that I helped build and nurture into an amazing force that could do anything. However, the writing was on the wall and a change for me was needed. So, I took over a new team

[2]   Matt Heller, *The Myth of Employee Burnout*, (The Peppertree Press, 2013). performanceoptimist.com

at a new company, which had people jumping ship before I even got there. They were some great individuals and they were wonderful at what they did—individually. However, they were terrible at working together.

Fast forward to less than a year later, and I have a team that's working so well together, I have people lined up from the last place I worked to be on my new team. So much so that someone from my last company that turned in their two-week's notice to come work for me, was offered the same position and pay that I was offering, to stay! (Higher pay than others in same position throughout whole resort.) They turned it down, giving further proof that pay is not the great motivator poor managers think it is.

That was the end of the first email. I couldn't let it end there... I had to know how!

The how was actually simpler than I thought it would be. One of the first things I did after being trained at their jobs and spending time on all three shifts with them, was to start 1-on-1's—dedicated time that each associate could spend with me, uninterrupted, each month. Very quickly I learned the problem was trust. Not that they thought the person next to them was a liar, but trusting that they were doing their job. Common phrases from my PBX operators would be, 'Front desk is out there doing X instead of Y!' Or 'PBX isn't picking up, because they are playing on their phones!' Even though they are all the same team, one department, they talked as if they didn't know each other.

So, several things had to happen. First everyone went through refresher training, so they all knew that everyone knew what to do and how to do it. Then they all spent two days shadowing other departments, learning what they go through (house-keeping, activities, F&B, engineering). Then, the segmented schedule became one giant schedule. Regardless of position or shift, we were going to be one team, even if only on paper.

Very slowly, I started rotating people into different positions. Though some were better or more comfortable in specific roles, I needed them to occasionally experience the rest of the department. This was the rough one, because no one likes their schedule messed with or going outside their comfort zone. So of course, I had a few ruffled feathers. Again the one-on-ones were key here. Positive and individualized encouragement helped those through the process. Change management 101, as well as opening the lines of communication. Simply encouraging each other to talk!

I also began hiring differently than my predecessor. Before, they hired experience and resumes. But I hire people and personalities. Hiring people I know would get along with the people I already have and be a part of my team. Which meant passing over very qualified candidates.

However, trust takes time. We've all lost trust in someone or something and only time will win that trust back. So, I could not force it overnight—which was the hardest part. Sitting back and telling my superiors and HR that it's working—just give it time. Looking back now, it didn't take too much time at all. In two months, my scores did a 180 and have been climbing ever since. In our score system, we celebrate single-digit increases, because it takes a lot to move that needle. I had increases of 15% points over previous months. In fact, my summer scores are the highest in the history of the resort. And they are the highest year-to-date. In the middle of the 100 days of summer, my team is crushing it. (By the way, I've not lost a single associate all summer.)

They are no longer focused solely on their individual jobs, but are helping those next to them. And even doing more work to make the next shift's job easier. I have associates seeking out MORE work to do on their own. Simply because the shift prior to them did the same.

Now there is more to it than just trust. Empowerment, empathy, etc. are all key elements to a great team, but the major issue at the start—simply trust."

To me, this story is a great example of what can be achieved if the proper judgment is used to balance leadership actions. Dallas balanced his need as a leader to have a productive team that would meet company goals with the needs of his team. They needed to be heard. They needed to be understood. And whether they liked it or not, they also needed to understand. It's not just about them.

So, trust couldn't be achieved WITHOUT balance.

Which brings me to an axiom related to balance that EVERY leader needs to understand and embrace:

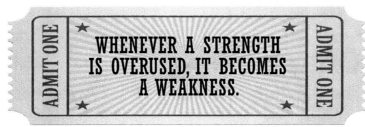

ADMIT ONE | WHENEVER A STRENGTH IS OVERUSED, IT BECOMES A WEAKNESS. | ADMIT ONE

Picture someone who values others' opinions. They ask a lot of questions before deciding, making sure that everyone has had their say. Great. People love to be heard.

However, now picture that same person struggling to make a decision or set a course, because too many of the people he asked had differing opinions, and he can't think of a way to make everyone happy. A decision is delayed until he can figure it out, all while his employees are getting frustrated and impatient.

Of course it works the other way, too. We've probably all known the Type A, take-charge type of manager. Their confidence allows them to "boldly go where no one has gone before." That's great in many cases, and they'll get a lot of people to follow them. What happens when they are wrong? What happens when their overconfidence manifests itself in a lack of preparation and innocent people suffer because of it?

In both cases, they were out of balance, and that's where these two concepts collide. Knowing yourself well enough that you know your strengths and weaknesses, but also having the awareness to balance out your behavioral tendencies to avoid negative, or incorrect, perceptions. Phew!

Chapter 9
The Inevitable Tipping of the Applecart

Super. You have learned about yourself, decided to actively balance your activities and attitudes, and are working on building trust, respect, and relationships.

Everything is going smoothly until ... someone upsets the applecart. If you made it an hour into your first shift as a supervisor before this happens, congratulations.

Who would upset the applecart, you ask? Who would throw a kink into your plan? The long and short of it is ... everyone. This chapter contains information about how to deal with some of the common and pesky applecart-flippers you will encounter. Let's start with a popular one.

Generations

How old are you? Are you older or younger than the people you lead? My guess is the answer is "both." You are now in charge of people potentially 30 or even 40 years your senior, along with employees who aren't old enough to drive, drink, or vote. Talk about balance!

If you are familiar with my take on the various generations at work, you know that I may not share the doom-and-gloom-outlook of some of my contemporaries. Some will say that there are so many differences in the generations that you would need a map, compass, GPS, and trained expedition guide just to navigate those waters. And while there are differences in the outlooks of people from various generations, focusing too heavily on that tends to further alienate the people we are trying to bring together.

In Chapter 7, we talked about how dangerous it can be to "generalize" about generational differences. As I stated then, I prefer instead to focus on our similarities, and how we as leaders can build relationships with the individuals to foster better teamwork, guest service, and business outcomes.

What do we ALL want, especially from a leader? Someone to listen to us, someone to help us, someone to notice our progress ... and to MAKE actual progress. Many people thrive on doing new things, learning new things, experiencing new things, and you can be the one who helps provide all of that to your employees.

To be fair, these may all look different to different people (never mind generations). So instead of pigeonholing an entire generation based on a few historical events, let's get to know the PEOPLE. Understand who they are and what they want. Only *then* can you deliver it!

Overachievers

We all want overachievers on our team, right? They are the ones who get things done and make their supervisor (you) look like a genius.

It's true that overachievers achieve a lot. They are generally easy to trust because they show you early on that they are trustworthy. They do what they say they will do and offer suggestions for improvement. Super.

They also require a bit more attention than you might think. If you can't implement a suggestion, they will want to know why (they aren't the only ones who want to know why, but they may be the most vocal about it). When they do this, they are not trying to be annoying, but they are truly trying to understand the process. So, tell them. Be upfront. If they have a great idea that is too expensive, tell them that. Don't make up some excuse or reason that sounds more palatable—tell them the truth.

But … don't just leave it at that. Your overachievers won't. They will want to know how they can move, change, or modify the process so they CAN get their idea implemented. If it truly is a good idea, why not let them try?

Give them some time and parameters and ask them to come up with a plan that will work within the real budget, time, or resource constraints you are facing. If it's an issue that will have to wait until next year, let them know that upfront, so they know what they are working toward.

Overachievers are also famous for topping-out when there are limited promotional opportunities. "Mikaela would make a great supervisor … she is great with people, has the technical know-how and loves the work we do. Too bad we don't have a spot for her."

This would often lead to Mikaela getting bored with her role ... she has mastered it and is ready to take on more responsibility, but we have nothing to offer her in terms of additional challenges. Even if you don't have an official leadership spot, what sort of projects or assignments can Mikaela take on to not only tap into her overachieverness for the company's benefit, but can also keep her interested and engaged so she doesn't start looking for work elsewhere?

Do you have cleaning crews? Daily or weekly meetings? Staff parties? Let Mikaela be in charge of one of those.

Do you need help with organizing or updating training materials or performing the training itself? Ask Mikaela to help.

For more on how and what to delegate, check out Chapter 11.

More responsibility doesn't always have to be about a promotion. It can also be a way to test your potential leaders to see if they really have what it takes to lead. We'll cover that in more detail later in the book.

Underachievers

Slacker. Lazy. Unmotivated. This is how many refer to those who consistently underperform our expectations. But here is the problem with those descriptors—they don't leave a lot of room to improve. They are judgments based on what we see, but they may not tell the entire story.

How many of you excelled in every class in school? If

you did, please see the section on overachievers. For the rest of us, there were likely some classes that we underperformed in, and some that we did well in.

Why is that? It's because for some reason, certain classes were more interesting to us than others. Maybe it was the subject matter, or an engaging teacher, or something about the environment or other students that helped to hold our attention. Whatever the reasons, my parents could always tell which classes I was underperforming in when the report cards came out.

One of our jobs as leaders is to assess why someone might be underachieving or underperforming. Is it their comfort level with the job or tasks, their interest in the work they are doing, or could it be something we did, didn't do, or overlooked that is impacting their working environment?

And since it's that last one (about us) that can have the largest impact, we should start our questioning there. Did we hire the right person for the right role? Did we adequately prepare and train them? Is it reasonable for us to believe that they SHOULD be performing up to standards? What road-blocks or obstacles have we not removed?

One of the most common reasons that underachievers do so is that they don't feel like they are making a valuable contribution to the big picture. They feel insignificant and like just another cog in the machine. That's where communication comes in ... by consistently reinforcing the standards and where people are in relation to those standards, we can show them their value and why what they do is so important (and who it's important to!).

If someone is underperforming because they are in the wrong role, what do we do about it? Let's say they aren't keeping up as a ticket seller. We'll assume for a moment that they have had adequate training, but their heart just doesn't seem to be in it. What if we gave them a chance to see how things are in another department? What if we found they weren't comfortable with guests, but rocked the house behind the scenes? We're not always going to get people in the perfect role right off the bat, but that doesn't mean they should be punished for underachieving or lost from the company altogether. We owe it to our employees, our guests, and our organizations to try to get people into roles where they will naturally flourish. Turnover rates are too high to just give up, send them on their way, and hope a rock star that you can easily place walks through the door.

Jerks

Yes, jerks. You know who I mean. They are NOT the well-intentioned overachiever who just wants to under-stand, and they are not the underperforming employee who just hasn't found their footing yet. They are ones who upset the applecart just for fun.

Or I should say, for the attention. What do we humans do when we don't get enough positive attention? We seek nega-tive attention. Really any attention will do at that point, just

97

to know we are alive and aren't alone. So an employee who is feeling isolated stirs the pot just to get people to notice him, and it usually works. Unfortunately, it may work a little too well, as that behavior will likely cause others to draw away even more. That then causes the jerks to be even more jerky.

Now, it's possible that someone is feeling isolated at work, and there could be things we've done (or are doing) to cause that isolated feeling. I do not want to discount this.

> *We must ALWAYS look at our own behavior first when deciding what is impacting someone else.*

That said, many of the jerks I have encountered in my time have been jerks from the word go. They didn't need any help from anyone at work. They brought that baggage with them.

If that's the case, if they truly value stirring the pot more than being a productive member of the team, it's time to cut ties and let them pursue other opportunities for employment. Don't keep them around because they are "good operators" or have great availability. If they are toxic to the team—they should be gone.

If you have ever played on a sports team, you know what I am talking about. The star running back may be fast, but if he is a jerk, no one will want to block for him. A player with less talent (but greater sense of teamwork) may actually outperform the star, because he has the support of those around him.

So often I hear leaders justify jerky or unproductive behavior by saying, "She is a great sales person—she sells more than anyone else. But no one will work with her, because she makes them miserable."

If you allow that person to stay so you can benefit from their sales prowess, then you are saying that the awful team behavior is okay. And that team behavior may be causing more harm than you can calculate on a balance sheet. Team dysfunction, gossip, turnover, lack of sales by others… the list goes on and on.

This is one of those long-term vs. short-term decisions that you have to make as a leader. If you have coached the employee about their team behavior, and they are just not coming around, it is probably better off, in the long run, to allow that employee to seek employment elsewhere. You may lose the sales for a short term, but in the long run, your employees will see that you value (and are willing to uphold) the behaviors that lead to strong team cohesion AND sales goals. Don't look now, but the concept of balance just made its presence known again.

Chapter 10
Go Forth and Lead –
Employee Relations and Development

We already know that your focus as a leader should be on your employees. What do they need? What can you provide? How can you support their development and create an environment where they want to stay employed with you AND perform at a high level?

Many books and articles have been written about the behaviors or characteristics of effective leaders. They have titles like, "The 8 Things Every Leader Does", or "15 Habits a Leader Must Develop (or break)." When you look closely at these lists, you often find overlap in the recommendations, but you also find some contradictions. Can leadership really be boiled down to a convenient list? p.65

I don't think so, but there are some guiding principles you can use that will give you an idea of how you should be spending your time in support of your employees. One of the best "models" I have found for this comes from MHI Global, a workplace training and research firm. In 2015, they sought to find the concepts, not the specific items on a list, which make leaders effective.

Their research uncovered four core capabilities that

when applied, lead to increased employee engagement, lower turnover, and better overall performance. Those core capabilities are:

MHI Global focused their efforts and research on the following industries:

- ▶ Finance
- ▶ Healthcare
- ▶ Manufacturing
- ▶ Business Services

Following is a description of each of the core capabilities and how I believe they apply to the attractions industry.

Involve

The late Al Weber, Jr. of Apex Parks Group (also formerly of Paramount and Six Flags) once said, "In order to keep the best people in your organization, you have to involve them. You don't have to agree, but you do have to involve them."

That quote has stuck with me for many years, because it speaks to a need of employees as well as a huge fear of many leaders.

Employees need to be heard—whether that is through informal conversations, targeted coaching, or an anonymous survey, it's human nature to feel valued when you know that your opinions are being listened to. And we have an obligation to not only listen when employees choose to speak up, but to also proactively seek out their input. We then need to do something with that input, but we'll address that in a few minutes.

First, I wanted to talk about the leadership fears that Al's quote eludes to ... disagreement. Disagreement is conflict, and conflict can be tough. When you willingly open the floodgates to others' opinions, you are most definitely going to get thoughts and feedback that don't line up with your own sensibilities or view of reality. That can be jarring even for the most seasoned leader. That's why many people shy away from putting themselves in a position where disagreements (a.k.a. conflicts) can arise. When you get into a leadership role, though, this is a daily occurrence. Developing the skills to deal with it should be a top priority.

That is, of course, if you intend to address the disagreements or conflicts. If you would rather stick your head in the sand, I wish you luck in whatever your next endeavor will be, because you won't last long as a leader. You may hold on to your leadership position because your boss also has his or her head in the sand, but you won't be very effective.

This reminds me of a leader I worked with many years ago (name and location withheld to protect the...

um … innocent). We were talking one day about what our employees wanted, and I said, "Why don't we do a survey? They can fill it out anonymously and that will give us an idea of what they want and what they think about us."

By his reaction, you would have thought I suggested that we walk down the midway naked at 2 p.m. on a Saturday. He was not having it.

"No way! We don't want to know what they think of us!"

And there it was … he didn't want to ask the question for fear of hearing the answer. If he heard an answer he didn't like, he was going to have to change or somehow justify continuing with his current behavior. At the time, he was very much of a rule-by-fear type of manager. You didn't develop personal relationships with your subordinates and you certainly didn't care about what they thought about you or your tactics. He was the manager, so he knew best.

In many ways, he taught me some of the finer points of employee relations—as in what not to do. Just like in many ways this book is dedicated to Patrick, because of what we put him through, it's also inspired by great and not-so-great leaders I have had in the past. Each one has taught me something different about the art of leadership. In this case, it was what *not* to put on the canvas.

And this brings us back to what to do if you do ask for involvement through a survey or even a personal request. Something must be done with the information you get back. Otherwise, what's the point of asking?

This does not mean you have to implement every idea or suggestion that is brought to you. That would be impractical and probably impossible. Instead, it's up to you and your management team to figure what is truly important, what will benefit the most people, how the idea might be implemented and what the cost might be. Some of those decisions may be beyond your scope, so those items will be up to your management team. That said, once this process is complete, you still aren't done.

It's critical the feedback comes full circle. This means that if you are acting on a suggestion, let your team know what actions you are taking and the timeline for completion (or when they might start seeing results of the efforts). Some ideas that take longer term planning will need to be put off until a different time. That's okay. Let people know your plans so they see that their input was heard and is making a difference.

repeat p. 94

If you can't or won't do something, explain that, too. Is it a budget issue? Was it too narrow in scope? Was it not in line with company values or other initiatives? Contrary to what many front liners might think, management does usually have some pretty solid reasons behind why they do what they do (or don't do). If that's not explained, however, employees will fill in the blanks.

If you are honest with your team about the criteria and parameters you used to come to a decision, this conversation can be a true teaching moment. You have the opportunity to share a real-life example of how management makes decisions. Wouldn't that be helpful in grooming future leaders?

One thing I would like to address here … what if you have no legitimate reason NOT to do something? What if it's just uncomfortable, new, or you are afraid your boss won't like it? If your reasoning boils down to, "We've never done it that way before," or "I just don't think it will work," please don't tell your employees that. Don't tell them that you are closed-minded and lazy. They may think that already, so no need to give them additional ammunition.

Instead, the challenge of leadership is to identify when it is time to try something new or uncomfortable. If you have the budget, the time, and the resources … why not?

This actually brings us to another opportunity for involvement. If the action needs a development team or some other input, why not get your employees to help?

Not only does this involve them, it also teaches them about leadership, business practices, and the steps it takes to implement an idea. I would guess that most front-line employees are blissfully unaware of how much effort, thought, and deliberation goes into every initiative. This would be a great chance to show them and even get them to take part in the process.

Involvement is about allowing your employees to use their brains and passions to help you succeed. Why wouldn't you want them to do that?

Encourage

Raise your hand if you have ever felt encouraged. Who was doing the encouraging? What did it feel like?

Since the word 'encourage' is defined as: *to inspire with courage, spirit, or confidence,* you likely felt empowered, strong, and even capable of things you didn't realize you could do. And I'll bet the person who was encouraging you was being supportive and patient, yet firm.

From my experience, there is a fundamental mindset that is common to those who consistently provide an encouraging environment for others … it's whether you focus more on what you can do versus what you can't do.

Think about an employee handbook. Most of them that I have seen focus on what not to do. Sure, there is some mention of the company values and a sentence or two about what that sort of means, but rarely have I seen the list of dos outnumber the list of don'ts. Even if it's subtle, this imbalance sets up the employee to think that they better keep their nose clean if they want to keep their job.

What if we looked at it the other way? What if we supplied our employees with a boatload of information about what they *could* do? I don't mean tasks or work assignments, because they are going to get that anyway. I'm referring to the often unwritten rules of engagement with your guests or fellow team members.

For example, let's say one of your organizational values is Teamwork. Great! In the handbook it says, "At Big Al's

Amusement Pier, we foster a strong sense of TEAMWORK in every interaction!"

That sounds mildly encouraging, but it doesn't give much direction on what that means to a new employee. What if you followed that up with some examples?

"At Big Al's Amusement Pier, we foster a strong sense of TEAMWORK in every interaction! Here are some examples of specific behaviors that support our value of TEAMWORK:

▶ Offering to help when others are in need—possibly covering a shift or assisting with a cleaning project

▶ Keeping all common areas (work spaces, breakrooms, storage areas) clean and organized for the next person

▶ Saying "please" when you ask for something and "thank you" when it's delivered.

Contrast this with what I have seen in most employee handbooks:

▶ Do not leave food or personal trash in the breakroom

▶ Do not leave cleaning supplies out and visible in guest areas

▶ Do not leave a shift open—if you cannot come in, it is your responsibility to find someone to take over

In which workplace would you rather spend your time?

I'm going to sound like John Lennon for a moment … but just imagine if your entire workforce offered help before being asked, consistently said please and thank you, and proactively kept their workspaces clean? That would reduce your headaches by what—90% or so?

And it all comes back to our approach—what CAN you do versus what you CAN'T do.

To be clear, I am not suggesting that just writing these things in your handbook is going make them magically appear. Quite the contrary. This is a starting point, a building block, a guidance system for employees and managers. This is NOT the end game.

In order for ANY written policy or direction to come to life, action must be taken. **By you.** Very few employees I have interacted with over the last 30 years have read the employee handbook cover to cover, memorized everything inside, and lived their work life 100% by the rules, policies, and guidelines contained therein. Just doesn't happen that way.

So if we are going to start with some encouraging, can-do statements and suggestions, we have to follow that up with encouraging, can-do behaviors. What are we doing each day to inspire with courage, spirit, or confidence?

I think the first question to ask and answer is: when is encouragement appropriate? In other words, when do people need to be inspired with courage, spirit, or confidence?

On one hand, you could argue that they need this all the time. That in order for employees to thrive, they need a steady stream of positive and encouraging vibes hurled in their general direction. I think this is true in small doses. Under typical circumstances, a well-timed "You can do it" or

"You've got this" (sincerely delivered) will be appropriate to get people over the next hurdle. Where I think real encouragement comes in is during times of high stress or intense activity, when a person's self-assurance may be lacking.

For example, if you are training someone on a new procedure, especially one that is more taxing or complex than what they have attempted in the past, this is a great time to be encouraging!

I remember specifically being trained on the Galaxi roller coaster when I was working at Canobie Lake Park. The Galaxi was a ride where everything was done manually, from dispatching the cars to setting brake pressures and knowing when to "pop," or open the brakes as the cars went through them to ensure a smooth slow-down for the guests. It was one of the most complex rides to operate in the park, and since it took so long to learn, only a small group of employees were given the opportunity to be "G-Men" every summer.

If there were two things that a Galaxi operator needed, they were courage and confidence. Courage to sit in the operator's chair and know that you were going to be able to successfully (and smoothly) stop a car full of guests every 45 seconds or so. And confidence that your judgment and training would pay off … that you would be able to assess the speed and weight of the cars, as well as the track and weather conditions so you could adjust the brakes to the right pressure and then activate them at just the right moment.

Sitting in that chair for the first time, you felt neither of those things.

So it took a lot of encouragement from the current staff and trainers to build up the new recruits. Some caught on quicker than others, but it was always an uphill battle. Here are some of the phrases I remember hearing during my training at the Galaxi:

- ▶ "Good job!"
- ▶ "See how smooth that was? You've got this."
- ▶ "Next time, try a little less pressure on brake 7"
- ▶ "You're doing great! How do you feel?"
- ▶ "That car had four large adults, you could have used more pressure on brakes 5/6, then popped it just as the fin exited the brake. You'll get it."
- ▶ "What questions do you have?"

Notice that this isn't just about the positive praise. Corrective actions, when delivered properly, can also be encouraging. When they said, "Next time," it meant that there would be a next time, and that I was on the right track. I wasn't there yet, but was moving in the right direction.

Years later, when I was working at Universal Orlando Resort in the training department, I had a leader named Kirsten Abbott-West. She used to tell us that our job was not only to build competence in terms of skills learned, but also to build in the confidence to go out and use those new skills. To me, that was about encouragement.

Sometimes encouragement is needed to get people over

an obstacle that they can't seem to clear on their own. In those cases, more of a coaching approach might be needed.

One of your employees, Scott, is having trouble interacting with guests. He is very personable with fellow employees in back-of-house areas, but when he gets in front of guests, it's almost like a switch is flipped and he turns into a different person.

A coaching conversation with him might go something like this:

You: *Scott, thanks for meeting with me. I wanted to talk about your interactions with guests. I've noticed that you have no trouble talking with employees and even joking around with them, but when you are with the guests, you seem to shut down. I don't see you make eye contact and you rarely smile.*

Scott: *I do my job, though. I have never been even a penny off in my till, and the line moves really fast when I am working.*

You: *You're right, you are great on the register and I am sure the guests appreciate how quickly they get through the line. That's only part of your job, though. You are also responsible for ensuring the guests feel welcomed and that we want them to come back. That doesn't always come across when you don't make eye contact or even smile at them.*

Scott: *Well, the guests seem angry if the line doesn't move fast enough, and I know how important it is for the money*

to be right, so that's what I concentrate on.

You: *That's all true, but what happens if the guests have a bad experience, or if an employee makes them feel like they are a bother?*

Scott: *They probably wouldn't want to come back.*

You: *Exactly. That's why we have to balance the speed at which we get people through the line and showing them some hospitality so they know that we care about them.*

         So if you were to think about going a little slower, what might you say to a guest as they came up to your register.

Scott: *Hi?*

You: *That's a great start. What else?*

Scott: *Did you find everything you were looking for?*

You: *Excellent! And what would happen if they told you that they hadn't found everything they were looking for?*

Scott: *I could tell them where it is?*

You: *Perfect—yes! And that would provide them an even better experience, right?*

Scott: *Right.*

You: *So how would you feel about giving that a try on your next shift?*

Scott: *I can do that, as long as the guests don't get mad, if the line is too long.*

You: *Sure. How about this ... how about if I am out there with you and we can look at the line together. Would that help?*

Scott: *Sure, that would be great.*

In this case, there were lots of opportunities for encouragement, and also a little digging to be done to figure out why this was such a roadblock for Scott. Turns out he already knew what he should have been doing, but he needed the courage and confidence it took to know that it would be okay to do those things.

We also see again that encouragement is not just about throwing praise at people. It's much more likely to be needed when things aren't going perfectly. You'll need to redirect a behavior, and also let them know that they CAN do it.

Develop

There is a reason that professional training and learning entities often add the word "development" to their departmental titles, for example, "Training and Development" or "Learning and Development."

The reason is that development is different than both training and learning, and it's a crucial part of the employee experience equation.

▶ We can train someone on the tasks of doing their job, but that doesn't mean we've developed them.

▶ Employees can learn about the different products we have to offer, but that doesn't mean they have been developed.

▶ Development is about growing and advancing your capabilities. Learning and training are a part of that process, but do not account for all of the moving pieces.

When I think of someone who has grown and developed, I think of someone who:

- ▶ Is now thinking differently (big picture or long-term)
- ▶ Takes additional viewpoints or data points into consideration
- ▶ Has a wider scope of influence
- ▶ Can connect the dots and balance multiple priorities

If you said, "Those sound like leadership qualities," you win the prize! We talked earlier about developing the Leadership mindset, and that comes through assessing things in a different way, judging situations with more dynamic data and being able to consider multiple angles to complex problems. Those skills don't just appear at the ready overnight. They need to be taught, honed, and developed.

So what does development mean for your employees? Heck, you probably still feel like YOU are being developed, and now you have to think about how to develop your employees? Jeepers!

The one tool in your arsenal that will help you with this is your ability to explain *Why*.

When something happens, whether it's a mechanical breakdown or an upset guest, it's important to explain to your employees, to the best of your ability, why it happened and why you are doing what you are doing to resolve it. Without this explanation, your employees' minds wander to all sorts of illogical conclusions.

This stunts the development process in two ways.

1. It doesn't present all of the pertinent and true information to your employees for them to consider

2. Once their "fill-in-the-blank" information takes hold, it's really tough to overcome that with the truth. We believe what we want to believe (and often it's the first thing we hear that takes hold).

That's why communicating the why is so critical, especially in developing the thought process of our employees.

Speaking of why, why should we be concerned with developing a different outlook in our employees? Why should it matter that they can think beyond their immediate tasks?

For starters, it creates engagement (the whole reason for this discussion). Since people don't like to stagnate, growing and developing allows people to feel like they are moving forward, which most people like and even crave. It also gives them a sense of purpose, and encourages them to buy into the purpose of your company. Just because we put up a poster with our mission statement on it does not mean that everyone understands it or supports it. Employees first have to see that we mean what we say (that we are truly living our mission) before they will decide that it's worth their time to embrace.

Unfortunately, there are far too many companies who have wonderfully crafted mission statements that don't mean anything in the real world. If an employee is coming to you from one of those companies, they will rightfully be skeptical of your mission statement until you prove that it's more than a bunch of five dollar words being asked to co-exist on a fancy poster in the breakroom.

What this also shows us is that this process of development takes time. You may have to explain "why" multiple times and in multiple ways. Until you find out what is important to your employees and what drives them, you may not know what the right approach is or what really "speaks" to them.

I have a friend who recently took a job that he was, in many ways, overqualified for. He said something to me the other day that I think we really need to be conscience of when it comes to development. He said, "It's like I just appeared on this planet when they hired me. They had no idea what my background was, what I could do, or how I could help. They just told me what tasks to perform and that was it."
His insight impacts development in two ways:

- First, we should be getting to know our teams to understand what they bring to the table and how they can use their talents and abilities on the job – that increases engagement, too!
- Second, we need to be aware of the roadblocks that others have potentially put in place that we now have to deal with.

If someone comes to us from a job where management allowed them to be late, then that's the "training" they are bringing with them. That training has likely formed habits, and if you know anything about trying to lose weight or quit smoking, you know that habits can be very difficult to break. But break them we must if we are going to help our employees build new, productive habits that work to our favor.

That's really what we are up against in so many areas of employee development—replacing potential bad habits with good ones. Since it can take up to three weeks to establish a new habit, you better get started right away with your new employees, unless you want them to develop new bad habits on your dime.

Guide

If you have even been on a road trip, you know how helpful a map, GPS, or compass can be. They keep you on the right path so you can get to your destination.

Our employees need that guidance as well. All employees are on a path; one that starts the day they get hired and ends the day they leave the company (for any reason). Our job, then, is to keep them on the right path and moving forward. We are the map, GPS, AND compass.

This is partly achieved through the example that we set. We've already discussed that you are a role model, and that your employees are watching. They will decide which way to go based on what they see you do. It might not even be something overt or obvious, but something subtle that they can interpret in their own way.

We also do this through feedback – timely conversations

that let people know how they are doing. Are they veering off the path, or are they doing great, even being able to pick up speed? Feedback allows people to see their behaviors through someone else's eyes, so they can gain insight and perspective into the impact they are having on others. Since employees don't always know what that impact is, it is up to us to guide them in the right direction.

There are a few elements of delivering feedback that need to be mastered to ensure that it's delivered effectively. This is one of those things you will mess up once or twice, even if you are seasoned at the process. We're dealing with human beings after all, and it's nearly impossible to accurately predict the way everyone will react when given information about their performance.

To best prepare yourself for giving feedback, it's a good idea to practice before you have to deliver it for the first time. Get a colleague or friend to sit with you and pretend to be an employee. Give them a situation and go through the steps of sharing the feedback. Just taking the time to find the words and to be able to think through the process will help you be ready for the real thing.

Here are the elements of feedback to be aware of and practice, so you can be as effective as possible:

▶ **Consider emotions** – before delivering the feedback, consider both the emotional state of the receiver as well as your own. If you are not both calm and ready to have a productive conversation, it may be best to postpose the conversation for a little bit. The only time this doesn't apply is when the safety of a guest or employee is involved. Safety is number one and must come before anything else. You can always explain your actions later (and you should), but when safety is concerned, every second counts.

▶ **Consider time and place** – even if the emotional box is checked, delivering feedback (positive or negative) at the wrong time and in the wrong place can reverse the outcome of your efforts. For corrective feedback, privacy is king. Want to see an employee get riled up and defensive? Deliver negative feedback about their behavior in front of their peers or coworkers. At the same time, some people get embarrassed even by providing positive feedback in front of others. Know who these people are on your team. Watch and listen for clues that will tell you which side of the feedback fence your employees are on. If they cringe when others get public praise, there is a chance they would not like to be in the same situation. Likewise, if they are outgoing and regularly put themselves in the spotlight, public praise may be what they crave.

▶ **Make it personal** – nothing is worse than a leader delivering "feedback" to the masses. "Thank you, everyone, you did a great job today!" Really? Did everyone really do a great job? You don't know, but you can check the feedback box, right? Wrong. Feedback is about speaking to an individual about what they specifically did that either upheld or fell below your standards of conduct. You can make it personal by making appropriate eye

119

contact, using their name and being specific about what they did and how they impacted someone else (either the team, a coworker, a guest, or the company).

▶ **Don't make it TOO personal** – giving feedback should not be an open invitation to demean a person. In fact, even corrective feedback should be delivered in a way that shows you are trying to help them improve, not belittle them for a short coming. Your feedback stays objective when you focus on the facts. What did you see or hear? What do you know to be true? Speculation, hearsay, and guesswork have no place in the feedback universe. A judge wouldn't allow them in a court of law, and you shouldn't let them into your feedback.

Ultimately, the questions you should be asking yourself before giving feedback are: What did the person do? How did that impact others? What company standard was upheld or violated? Your feedback should answer those questions.

Here's an example of positive feedback:

You've just walked by your ticket selling team and noticed that Gina is consistently asking people where they are from and how long they are planning to stay. This is something that you ask all ticket sellers to do to find out what the best ticket packages will be for that guest.

When Gina has a free second, you step over to her station.

"Gina, I noticed how you consistently ask where people are from (what she did). That's awesome! I'm sure the guests appreciate being able to get the right ticket package for their experience (impact on guests). That really helps us achieve our goal of personalized service for every guest (company standard). I appreciate your efforts!"

Here is an example of what it would sound like if Gina wasn't meeting the standard:

You: *"Gina, I noticed that you are not asking guests where they are from or how long they are planning to stay when they come to buy tickets" (what she did).*

Gina: *"Yeah, I guess I forget sometimes when it gets busy."*

You: *"This is actually when it's most important. Since the museum will be crowded today, we want to make sure the guests get to do everything they came to do. By asking about their schedule now, it can save them a lot of time later on" (impact on guests).*

Gina: *"Okay, I'll make a point to ask every guest."*

You: *"Great! They all deserve our best personalized service (company standard). Thanks, Gina!"*

Notice that the feedback for improvement included more of an opportunity for a response from the employee. That refers back to the need to consider emotions … dumping all of this on an employee at once without giving them an opportunity to defend themselves isn't fair, and can escalate the situation quickly. Does this also sound similar to the process of encouragement we discussed earlier? It should, because it is.

Now, I want you to get a stopwatch and go back and read those examples of feedback again and see how long they take. Granted, there will be some variable with corrective feedback and the responses from your employees, but on the whole this doesn't take very long. As is, they both take less than 30 seconds. 30 SECONDS to guide and encourage your employees. You can make time for that, right?

There are also more informal occasions for guidance when you see or hear something that just doesn't sit right. As you involve your employees and ask their opinions, you may get into conversations where they share a perspective about something that just happened, maybe a management decision that they didn't agree with. They may say something like, "Management doesn't even think about us. They cut the budget without even considering how it would affect us."

You know this is not actually the case. You know (because you were in the meetings) that management actually did very carefully consider the impact this decision would have on the frontline employees. In fact, a number of managers held up the final decision as they tried to brainstorm ways to fix the financial issues without cutting the budget.

Because you know this, you have the opportunity to gently redirect this employee's perception. "I know having fewer people on staff isn't ideal, but we went back and forth about how to accomplish this without cutting the budget. We even asked a number of employees for their perspectives. In the end, there was a consensus that it was better to lower the hours of everyone, rather than having to let people go outright. This way when we can increase the hours back to where they should be, we'll still have all these good people on staff."

In that statement, you empathized with what they were going through, let them know what was behind the decision, and how you saw it playing out in the future. Notice that again we stuck to facts; this is what happened and why. This is not the time to get into an argument with your employees or try to convince them that your position is correct. They have every right to feel the way they feel, and it will take some time for the new information from you to sink in and be accepted. Best to leave it as it is and not force it. Your employees will feel you trying to strong arm them into believing something they are not yet ready to accept and will hold that against you.

We also have to be very careful in those situations not to over-promise a solution. In trying to make our employees feel better, it could be very easy to say, "Yep, we're going back to the normal schedule next week and in fact we'll all get even more hours!" You walk away the hero, feeling good that you delivered such good news.

But what happens when the next schedule comes out and the hours aren't back? You are now a liar and are not trustworthy. And... the employee now thinks they can lead better than you. How many of you saw that coming?

It's important to remember that this section is called "guide", not dictate, command or decree. Humans like to explore and find their own way. Sure, there are times when it's easier or more convenient to be told what to do, but when you get comfortable and start to see beyond the task in front of you, your brain starts to explore alternatives. We need at least a little bit of freedom and autonomy to remain sane. It's just how we're wired.

Chapter 11
Go Forth and Lead –
Action Management

For this section, we will not discuss the particular administrative tasks that come with being a leader – the specifics of which can be different at each company. Instead, we will focus on how to manage those tasks, balance your time, and develop leadership skills within yourself. To do this, we will cover four critical topics: Time Management, Delegation, Meetings, and Managing Up.

Time Management

From the get-go, we do have to acknowledge that there are certain administrative tasks that are daily realities in a leaders' life. Many new leaders struggle with finding the time to get all those things done AND get to know their team so they can truly lead them. With that in mind, let's start by talking about time management.

To me, time management is the wrong title. We cannot manage time. We cannot change time. An hour is an hour and a day is a day, and we all have the same number of each. Yet, some people consistently seem to get more done than others.

I prefer the term "action management" as this more

accurately describes what we are doing. We are managing the actions we take in a given period of time. We choose what we do and how we spend our time. Once we are able to embrace that concept and take control of our time-related choices, we'll be the ones setting the examples for efficiency!

When it comes to HOW to manage your actions, there are a bevy of systems and tools out there to help you do just that. Whether it's a calendar reminder on your phone, an app that keeps track of your to-do list or a post-it note on your computer monitor, you must pick the system that is right for you. But make no mistake, you do need a system.

If you are new to managing your OWN tasks and actions as a new leader, I would encourage you to experiment with various methods. Try several different tactics and see what works for you. Ask those over-achievers who never miss a deadline what they do, how they do it, and why they do it a certain way. Work on implementing a few simple ideas at a time and see what works for you.

As you can probably tell, I don't believe there is a one-size-fits-all solution, nor do I subscribe to one particular time ... er, action management method, and neither should you. Whatever system you use, it must be something that you can do, will do, and want to do. Don't take on a system or tool that makes managing your actions MORE cumbersome. That defeats the whole purpose.

Here are a few of the tactics that I have adopted over the years that have really helped my productivity.

Combine activities

As a supervisor at an attraction, you probably walk a lot; from one end of the property or building to the other and back again. Unless you have perfected teleportation, all that walking takes TIME. If you have two things to do at the one end of the facility, and in between you have traversed the property twice, you are potentially wasting a lot of time. If possible, when there are multiple things to do in the same area, do them at the same time and save the back and forth trips.

As an example, when I was in charge of the front gate at Valleyfair, there was paperwork that needed to be completed every morning that was a carryover from the day before. For the most part, they were refund requests from guests that the Guest Services staff had processed, and I needed to fill out the proper forms for our accounting department. In order to process those forms in a timely manner and issue the refund for the guests, the accounting team needed them by noon. Some of you may already see the dilemma … the morning is a critical time at the front gate, and as the manager I really wanted to be up there to support the team. So, I had a choice … process the forms in my office and not be at the front gate for opening, or risk not getting the paperwork to accounting by noon, therefore delaying the refund to the guest.

Or, I could pick Door Number 3. Instead of choosing between two sub-par options, I combined both activities. In the morning I would grab the paperwork and head up to the front gate. There was a small office just off the Guest Services area where I could fill out the forms while also listening to what was going on in Guest Services and keeping an eye on the operation. It was a win-win-win!

Combining activities like this takes planning. You have to know what you need to be doing and when those things need to be done.

Document things you don't want to forget

It sounds so simple, but just by writing the things down that I had to do helped me stay organized and gave me a framework for managing what I did throughout the day. Back in my day, I had two major tools that I would use to document important information: a pen and paper, and the phone.

When using the pen and paper method, I would simply make sure I had a pen and a piece of blank copy paper (folded in 1/8ths so it fit in my shirt pocket) before I went out into the park. As things came up, i.e. a request from an employee, a guest issue to follow-up on, a phone call that I needed to make, a maintenance request to check up on, or a supply order to be placed, I would write them all on that sheet of copy paper.

If it was a longer message or it needed more detail, I would find a nearby park phone and call my own voicemail. I would leave myself a message, then retrieve it when I got back to the office.

The items on the paper and the voicemails to myself became my to-do list, and it was EXTREMELY satisfying to cross things off the list as I did them. (Nothing wrong with playing these little psychological games to keep you on track!)

The important thing wasn't HOW I was documenting these things, it was THAT I was documenting these things. It was a system that was convenient, simple and sustainable ... something I could and would do because I saw that it was effective.

Some of the items that ended up on my to-do list could be taken care of right away, others required going to see certain people, making phone calls, inquiries, etc. But now at least I had a list.

Once one side of the page was full, I would refold the paper to reveal a blank side and start over.

Today, methods to document these ideas and tasks are more plentiful (and often electronic) but the concept is the same. Open a note on your phone, send yourself a text or email, download an app... again the method is less important than the action of doing it.

Besides not letting things fall through the cracks, there is one more benefit of documenting these things in the moment. When you write something down, or send a note, etc., you are telling your brain that you can file this away and won't need it for random access. That frees up your brain to allow other things in and to be more focused in the moment.

Urgent versus important

I mentioned earlier that once I have my list, I decide what I need to do and when. Many people struggle with deciding what order to do things, so the default order could be what's easy, who yelled loudest or who asked for a response first. By using the urgent versus important formula, you can develop more concrete criteria for scheduling the actions you are going to take.

If something is urgent, there is a high level of time-sensitivity. For example, an emergency stop at a ride is urgent, but you wouldn't necessarily put that on your schedule. It happens, and you react to it. On the other hand, providing timely processing of guest refunds is something you can put on a schedule, AND has a high level of time sensitivity. Things that you can schedule and have a high level of time sensitivity should go to the top of your list.

The other part of this formula is what is important. In this context, important refers to what is meaningful to the company. Again, processing refunds for guests is meaningful to the company, so that would qualify as important.

How do these two relate? Actions can be time sensitive AND meaningful to the company. But, they can also be non-time sensitive and meaningful to the company or, they can be time-sensitive, but not very meaningful (or less meaningful than something else). Using these relationships can help you decide what actions to take.

As you formulate your list, determine HOW urgent and HOW important a particular task or action is. For example:

▶ If it rates high on the urgent scale but low on importance, this means there is a tight deadline but the action is not (or may not be) meaningful to the company. This may not be a good use of your time.

▶ If it rates low on the urgent scale but high on importance, this is something that must be done, just not right now. Schedule this for later in the day or the week.

▶ If it rates high on urgency AND importance, take care of this first!

▶ If it rates low on urgency and low on importance, evaluate if you need to do it at all. This may be more of a waste of time than anything else.

As you read through those, I hope you were thinking of tasks and assignments you've had in the past that might fall into one of these categories. Now you can address future actions proactively to save time and be more productive.

All of the above tactics are geared toward the new things you will be doing. However, as a leader, a large portion of your role is the ability to get things done *through others*. Once the Leadership mindset is accepted and established, it will also be critical to develop the skill that eludes many new and seasoned leaders …

Delegation

Just saying that word in front of a group of leaders elicits a strong reaction. Either people have tried it with mixed or negative results, or there are too many variables to navigate to make it worth the effort. As a starting point for HOW to delegate (and better manage your actions), let's examine some of the typical reasons people say they don't delegate.

▶ **Takes too much time.** I get it. To delegate means to train, guide, follow-up, explain, communicate, follow-up again and then explain some more. If it's a task you are intimately familiar with, it would be much faster just to do it yourself. But news flash, that's not your job anymore. Your job is now to prepare others to be successful, and you do that by training, guiding, following up, communicating … see where this is going? In other words, delegating IS your job. Granted, it takes more time up front, but you will more than make up for it in the long run AND you will be developing your team (which is something they want anyway).

▶ **I enjoy doing (insert task here).** That's great, but see previous reason. That's not your job anymore. You can still do it (whatever it is) on occasion, but it shouldn't be part of your daily routine.

▶ **They won't do it exactly like I would.** GOOD! No one progresses by doing the same thing over and over again. Giving people the opportunity to put their own spin on something not only increases THEIR ownership, but might also uncover a new, more efficient or more productive way to do something. Don't fall into the trap of thinking that your way is the only way. It's not.

▶ **The last time I delegated, they screwed it up.** It's entirely possible that this is your fault as much (and maybe more) than it is theirs. Either you didn't prepare them well enough, follow up enough, or maybe you even picked the wrong person. Delegation is NOT just about telling someone to do something once and hoping it gets done correctly. Delegation is a development tool, not something you do and check off a list.

▶ **I don't know how.** Great! Admitting it is the first step!

While there are plenty of reasons (excuses) we don't delegate, there are even more important reasons TO delegate:

▶ **Develop staff** – by getting them to stretch and try new things, you get them to expand their thinking and skills. That's not only good for them, it's good for you and the company, too.

▶ **Saves your time** – if done correctly, delegating takes things off your plate that really shouldn't be there. It frees you up to focus on tomorrow's issues instead of putting out the fires of today.

▶ **Move forward** – with a developed staff and more time for you to focus on leading into the future, you now have the opportunity to truly move your business forward.

The next question that pops up is WHAT do I delegate? How do I know what tasks or projects to assign to other people? Let's answer those questions with a few more questions.

► "Does this HAVE to be done by me (or by someone in my position)?" If the answer is no, delegate it.

► "Is this something that will help others learn and grow?" If so, delegate it.

► "Does this involve sensitive or proprietary information, such as financial data?" If so, consider what information CAN be shared and whether or not that is enough to delegate. If not, keep it.

► "Does this involve confidential information about another employee?" If so, keep it.

Here are some examples:

► Planning an employee party – delegate it.

► Developing a recognition program – delegate it.

► Leading a meeting or training session – delegate it.

► Organizing a cleaning crew – delegate it.

► Developing new customer loyalty initiatives – delegate it.

► Analyzing workflow and efficiency – delegate it.

► Brainstorming ways to increase sales – delegate it.

▶ Recognizing employees for outstanding performance – keep it.*

▶ Coaching an employee on sub-standard performance – keep it.*

▶ Paperwork and reports – keep it.*

▶ Terminating an employee – keep it.*

* *These items absolutely belong to you. However, if you are developing an up-and-coming leader, they can shadow you and be a part of the process to learn, but that's different than delegating the task to someone else.*

This is not an all-inclusive list, but it should give you an indication of the types of things that you can delegate versus the things you must do yourself. That said, we shouldn't think that our list just shrank from eleven items to four. On the contrary, we still have responsibility over the seven things we're going to delegate, but that responsibility has changed. We go from DOING it to helping others learn how to do it.

Now that we know the obstacles (our own excuses), the reasons we should delegate and what to delegate, let's talk about the HOW.

The following tool may look familiar to those who have studied goal setting in the past. The S.M.A.R.T. model has been used for years to set, keep, and achieve personal and professional goals. Since delegation is partly about setting and achieving a goal, it makes sense to use it in this context, with a slight twist.

The S.M.A.R.T.E.R.
Model for Delegating

S pecific

The task or project you are delegating needs specifics to make it work. What specifically do you want someone to do? Some of those details will be filled in with the other parts of the model, but communicating a specific desired outcome will be critical from the beginning of the process.

M easurable

How will you know you completed something without a measurement? This could be a quantity of items produced, a successful event, or increased sales. For example, if delegating the planning of a party, you could say that you would like all departments involved, three different types of food and three activities that will appeal to all employees. These specifics give targets to work toward, keep things on track as you plan the party, and provide a measurement of success when completed.

A chievable

This one is largely dependent on the task being delegated and the people doing it. Is what you are asking able to be done in the allotted time with the allotted people and resources? Analyze that before giving the task. If it's not achievable, you are just setting your teams up to fail.

R elevant

Is the task or project relevant to the employee, to the job, to other team members or to the company? In other words, what's the WHY driving this? As much as you explain WHAT you want someone to do, it's just as critical for you to explain WHY they are doing it.

Timed

Every goal has an end point, and your delegated assignments should, too. If planning a party, you have the date of the party as a deadline. You could also set-up milestones along the way to check in. Three weeks out—has the food been ordered? Two weeks out, have the decorations been decided on? One week out, is all of the entertainment ready to go? This way you have progress points to help you see if things are on track. And, you aren't waiting until the morning of the party to find out nothing has been done! Having these check points also allows you to discuss other roadblocks that might have popped up that need to be dealt with.

Evaluate

Along with your check-in points, you will evaluate how the process is going AND the end result. If you asked for three food items and only two were delivered, a conversation with the employee or team responsible is necessary. This holds them accountable to what was expected and gives them an opportunity to learn and grow for next time.

Recognize

Acknowledge and encourage people's effort along the way by thanking them and being positive about their progress. When the project is done, recognize the accomplishments of the people involved—and be sure to be conscience of what type of recognition each person appreciates. Not everyone likes public praise, and if that's all you do, you could actually discourage someone from taking on a project like this in the future.

You are now probably wondering, "Exactly how does this save me time?" Delegating can and will remove certain things from your to do list, however it will add things that are more in line with what you should be doing anyway as a leader. It's ironic, but to have time to delegate (and by extension lead properly) you must delegate!

And here's the things that ties all of these action management concepts together. As a leader, your job is to look ahead and to have a plan for what's coming. This way, you can delegate, train or generally prepare your team to take care of things. That's why as a leader who manages their actions, you have to think about when you think about today.

Huh?

As a frontline employee, your thoughts were likely, for the most part, in the moment. Which meant that from a work standpoint, you thought about June 25th on June 25th, and that's fine. That's where and when we need you thinking about June 25th.

However, a leader can't afford to wait until June 25th to think about June 25th. If they do, they are going to be too late and there is a good chance, they will miss something. Like a picnic.

Early in my days at Valleyfair, I had not yet developed the habit of looking ahead at the picnic and company outing schedules. I wasn't in Food & Beverage, so you may ask, "What's the big deal?" The big deal is that once all of that food and beverage is consumed, there is a considerable clean-up to be done, and it was my staff in Park Services who took care of that.

On one particular Saturday, I was meeting with my Park Services supervisors, working out some issues we were having with communication. What I failed to do before this meeting was to look at the needs of the picnics and outings that day ... it was going to be WAY busy, meaning we would need additional staff in the picnic grounds, especially to clean and turnover the pavilions between groups. Unfortunately, when the first groups were finishing up and extra staff and supervision were needed, we were nowhere to be found.

Which is when the frantic radio calls and phone calls started. All at the same time we were hearing from catering managers, group sales representatives and the Marketing Director. You can imagine that none of them were super pleased about our lack of support. Trash cans were overflowing which created additional debris around the pavilions. This was my fault, and they were right to be upset.

Of course we all scurried down to the picnic grounds to play catch up as best as we could. It wasn't pretty, but in the end, we got everything back on track.

And that was my lesson on when leaders need to be thinking about today. Had I thought about and planned for that day two weeks prior, that situation wouldn't have happened. We would have had the staff in place and I never would have called a meeting of the troops when we should have been concentrating on the picnics.

The time between today and when you think about today grows exponentially as you climb the lift hill ... or leadership ladder. As a supervisor, you are probably thinking or looking a week or two out. A manager, probably one to three months. A director, six months to a year, and anyone considered an executive is looking multiple years down the road. That means that an executive probably thought about June 25, 2017 and what it was going to take to be successful back in 2014 or so. Wow.

This is why action management and delegation, specifically, are so important to a leader. You have to be able to figure out what it's going to take to be successful far into the future, and that takes time.

Meetings

Another factor of moving up the ladder is the number of meetings you will attend. Meetings can be great for collaborating, sharing ideas and even building camaraderie. Unfortunately, meetings can also devolve into gut-wrenching, mind-numbing, soul-sucking wastes of time. To avoid the latter (as you climb the ladder!), here are some tips both as the meeting organizer/leader and attendee.

Meeting organizer/leader

▶ **Define the reason for the meeting** – the focus of the meeting will be different if the time spent is for training on a new policy or a weekly information share. Always keep in mind, "What do we want/need to accomplish with this meeting?" If you can't come up with something, don't meet.

▶ **Invite the right people** – nothing is worse than being in a meeting you didn't need to attend… with the possible exception of not being at a meeting you should have attended. If you are responsible for who will be there, ensure you have ALL the right people or departments represented, and none that you don't. Not sure? Ask the people you THINK should be there. If they decline, because it doesn't pertain to them, no problem.

▶ **Have an agenda** – and stick to it! An agenda is your roadmap to make sure that the reason for having the meeting in the first place is accomplished. It helps keep you on track (if you stick to it) and by preparing it ahead of time, gives you an opportunity to make sure you don't forget anything (and, as a bonus, gives you a chance to think about all the people that might need to be there).

▶ **Set a timeframe** – and stick to that, too! Be ~~conscience~~ *conscious* of people's time by starting and ending when you said you would. If, when preparing your agenda, it looks like you have too much to cover in the allotted time, save it for another meeting or find another way to get

141

that information to the people it needs to get to. So what is a good timeframe? If this is a daily or weekly informational meeting: 10-15 minutes. If you'll be discussing things and possibly setting a course of direction: 45 minutes to an hour – tops! Usually the shorter the better, but you also want to plan enough time to discuss things and get input from others. Whatever your timeframe – stick to it! Once you say it's going to be 45 minutes, people will be looking at the clock at 35 minutes wondering if you'll be able to get through the next ten points on your agenda in the next 10 minutes.

▶ **Stay in control** – One of the reasons meetings go south is because one person rambles on incessantly about inane drivel that no one cares about—and the meeting leader does nothing to stop it. In fact, sometimes it IS the meeting leader! In order to stick to the agenda and stick to the timeframe, you as the meeting leader must be the one to keep things on track. That means politely being able to let someone know that it's time to move on to another topic. It could also mean playing peacemaker with employees who have vastly different opinions and who don't mind enthusiastically sharing those opinions at every turn. Once you let either of these situations (or the other thousand things that can derail your meeting) take over, you've lost. And your meeting sucks. And no one will want to come to another one.

▶ **Follow-up** – Meetings were never intended to be one-and-done endeavors, but because many turn out that way, they are not as productive as they could be. If a decision is made or a project is assigned, the end of the meeting should actually be the beginning of the follow-up process. Set a time in the near future to discuss progress and see if any assistance or support is needed. Put those assignments as the first agenda item for your next meeting—this shows people you were serious about getting results, not just talking about them.

Meeting attendee

► **Show up** – on time and prepared. Never be the reason someone has to say, "Let's give him a few more minutes." As a meeting leader, you should start on time, and as an attendee you should be ready to go on time. If there was something you were supposed to do, read, prepare, etc., get it done. Period.

► **Help keep things on track** – I worked with a guy once who was great at steering the conversation back to where it should have been, especially when the meeting leader got in the weeds of the discussion. He would say something like, "I think we're getting off topic" or "It sounds like we are talking about two different things." I know the meeting leader was always grateful for his assistance!

► **Contribute, don't dominate** – Share your ideas, be a part of the discussion, let people know about your observations; all within the context of a healthy

143

discourse. Avoid, at all costs, being the self-important windbag who just likes to hear themselves talk. If you don't know if that's you (and most windbags are blissfully unaware) watch the body language of the other people in the meeting. Are they rolling their eyes, looking at their phones, sitting back uninterested, yawning or staring blankly at you or the wall? Chances are you have achieved windbag status. Game over.

Meetings are living, breathing, organisms, but are rarely treated with the attention they deserve. They need to be fed, nurtured and guided to be healthy and productive. Otherwise, they become a beast the no one can tame.

Managing Up

To me, there is no more important aspect to leadership than nurturing positive relationships, and this includes how you interact with your direct supervisor. The rapport between the two of you can have a huge impact on the actions you take and how you use your time. It can also be the difference between a bridge and a brick wall.

Let me explain.

Very often, you are tasked with sharing information up or down the chain of command. You may be telling your frontline team members about a new promotion or product offering, or relaying feedback to your supervisor about how the team is dealing with a new procedure. Whatever the case, you are the conduit. You are the carrier of information. You get to determine who knows what and when. It's a big responsibility.

Used wisely and effectively, that responsibility can build a strong bridge between your supervisor and the front line. Open and honest communication on both ends keeps the information flowing and no one is in the dark, or made to fill in the blanks with their own assumptions. When not used appropriately, i.e. when we sugar coat things, leave out distressful details, or are less than forthright, we become a brick wall. We are the divide between our supervisor and the frontline. We are the information barrier that doesn't allow either side to fully know what's going on. This often leads to time wasted on worry and fear rather than figuring out how to move forward.

Here's an example of the brick wall:

During my time working in the training department of a large theme park company, I had the pleasure of supporting a number of different departments. In doing so I would attend operational meetings at all levels. One day, I was at a Director's meeting, and immediately went to one of his department manager meetings right after. What I heard kind of amazed me.

At the first meeting, the Director (we'll call him Roger) was talking about the use of overtime for frontline staff. I remember specifically what he said about it … "paying overtime can get expensive, and we'd like to avoid using whenever possible. However, it's important to realize that the service we provide our guests is our number one priority, and if we have to incur some overtime to have the right team members in the right places for our guests, then that's what we have to do. All I ask is that you give me a heads-up about how much you think you'll need and why."

I thought that was pretty reasonable. Don't use it if you can avoid it, but err on the side of guest service if it must be used. Apparently, I heard it differently than one of his department managers (we'll call him Brad).

I walked with Brad to his meeting, and took a seat as everyone else was getting settled. Brad and I had just come from the same meeting, and I expected to hear him repeat the things that Roger had talked about for the benefit of his supervisory staff.

And for the most part, he did… until he got to the topic of overtime. Knowing it was a sore subject with the supervisors, I was encouraged by what Roger had said. They had been complaining that their hands were tied by not being able to use a little overtime here and there and that guest service was suffering. I was kind of excited as I anticipated their jubilee of Roger's overtime decree.

Apparently, Brad heard the message differently, or decided that he needed to send a different message to his *staff. As he broached the overtime subject, this is what he said.*

"There is to be NO overtime used."

Wait, what? Were Brad and I at the same meeting? The frustration in the room was palpable as his supervisors let that little nugget of inspiration sink in.

And there it was ... the brick wall. Maybe unwittingly, Brad had laid the foundation for a barrier that would come between the supervisors and Roger. The supervisors would now judge Roger's ability to lead and understand their role on the fact that he couldn't seem to understand this one simple tenant of business—you have to have people to serve your guests. He was further hampering their ability to do their jobs with unrealistic directives and was more concerned with saving a few bucks than providing a quality guest experience.

Few things that I know of rile up the supervisory troops more than tasking them with providing a great guest experience and then cutting off their means to do so.

What's the fallout for Brad? He is supposed to be the supervisor's advocate. Surely he explained to Roger how important a little overtime would be and how it would have a positive impact on the guest experience, right? The supervisors likely feel that either he didn't do that, or didn't do it well enough. He will now have to spend his time explaining and re-explaining his point to his confused and disgruntled staff, rather than working with them to provide the best guest service possible.

The supervisors may also lose a little trust in Brad. Maybe he's not the advocate they thought he was? Maybe he doesn't work as hard for us as we thought? Maybe we don't need to work as hard for him …

And there it is. The impact of hitting the brick wall. Crash.

My question is—why the different messages? Why did Brad feel it was necessary to drop the hammer with the "no overtime" directive, knowing that; A) that's not what Roger said, and B) his supervisors really wanted to be able to use a little overtime? I think it had to do with two things that indicate a breakdown in the relationship between Brad and Roger.

Trust and Fear.

I don't think Brad trusted his supervisors enough to allow them to run with Roger's overtime instructions. He probably feared that they would use way too much and he would be in the awkward position of explaining that to Roger.

I also think Brad may not have trusted that Roger would have backed him up when the overtime was actually needed. Brad may have thought, "Well, that's what he is saying now, but wait until we actually need to use it. He'll be saying something different then." With that perception, Brad's fear of retaliation is warranted. However, how true is that perception? We may never know.

What we do know is this one action, stating that no overtime was allowed, had larger ramifications than Brad could have possibly realized. Roger may be happy that no overtime is used, but he really won't be happy when service starts to slip, and it's because the right people weren't in the right places at the right time. He's going to come looking for answers, and Brad better be ready.

And so it goes … the complex relationships created by the various levels and responsibilities within a company. On the surface, Brad and Roger got along well, were on the same page and supported the same things. Clearly when you dig into it, something else was happening behind the scenes.

Of course, the key to any relationship is communication. And the process of "managing up" or managing the relationship you have with your boss is no different. Just because you are the "subordinate" doesn't mean you can't influence and help drive how that relationship develops. In fact, it's in your best interest to do so.

Here are some things to consider when trying to strengthen the bond between you and your boss:

▶ **How does my boss communicate?** Do they communicate with a lot of detail, are they a storyteller, do they tend to listen more than speak, or do they speak rapidly and make quick decisions? Adapting to their style, or giving them the type of communication they appreciate, will help build the bridge.

▶ **What is it like in my boss' world?** What sort of challenges do they face? What keeps them up at night? What are the criteria that determine success at their level? Understanding these factors can give you insight into what they do and why, which will ultimately strengthen the relationship.

▶ **How can I help make that better?** Your boss is counting on you to help them succeed, just like your success is determined by the performance of your staff. How can you help your boss with their challenges? By definition, your tasks already support their initiatives, but how can you take that a step further? How can you be the person that seeks out proactive ways to make your boss' world run a little smoother?

▶ **What does my boss need from me?** I think that starts with trust and respect, and branches out to honest communication, direct feedback and getting things done. The best way to find out what your boss specifically needs from you is to ask. If you meet regularly, ask them periodically how you are doing with delivering what they need from you.

▶ **What do I need from my boss?** Do you need guidance, support, communication, and training? Do you need a sounding board? The big question is, do they know what you need? You may assume that since they've been in a leadership role for a while that they know what you need, but they probably don't. At least, not specifically until they get to know you a little better. If your boss doesn't sit down with you early on to discuss what you need and what they need, I would suggest requesting time to have that conversation. Be honest about what you expect and give them a chance to openly talk about what that will look like.

The relationship you have with your boss can make or break your experience. We hear all the time that employees don't leave companies, they leave bosses. And while you have to know what that means for you as someone who is leading others, you also have to know what that means to you as someone who is being led. Be a bridge, not a brick wall.

This entire chapter has been about the new things you'll be doing in your role as a leader. Managing your time differently, managing relationships differently, and carrying yourself differently—all because you got this promotion. It's not just about a new title and a new wardrobe, in fact those are the least of your worries. You are now acting on the behalf of others, influencing others and getting things done through others.

It's a big responsibility AND a never-ending journey. Don't get down on yourself if you make a mistake or don't do things perfectly at first. That's part of the process. You may be good at a lot of things, but few leaders are really good at all of the elements of leadership right out of the gate. Give yourself some time to learn, to grow, and let things sink in. But not too much time—you've got a job to do.

There's that balance thing again.

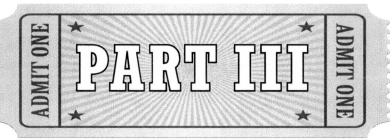

Arms Up!

Management Tools for
Developing New Leaders

To this point, we have focused on this transition and process from the new leader's perspective, with some insight peppered in here and there for their employers. The second part of this book tackles the other side of the equation. What do employers need to do to help new leaders navigate this process?

Just because we have changed directions a bit, this is no time for our new leaders to stop reading. This section will also benefit you by showing what it takes to develop a new leader (something you may already be charged with), as well as give insight into your own development process.

We will break down this section into three major categories:

1. **Selecting Right People**
2. **Training Appropriate Skills**
3. **Supporting a New Leader's Growth & Development**

Chapter 12
The Three Musketeers
of Leadership Development

While working with a client a few weeks ago, I had an epiphany. I recognize that this light bulb moment for me might indeed be a 'duh' moment for others, but either way, it's a valid illustration of the relationship of actions and activities required to develop leadership skills in others.

The property I was working with had a very old, but very well-maintained carousel. It's only one of two in the country (to my knowledge) that still has the brass ring machines that you could reach for while you ride. How cool is that?

What occurred to me one day was that the folks who built the carousel—the craftsmen, architects, builders, and electricians—are all gone. Even the people who ran it those first few seasons, working out the bugs and getting it to run smoothly, are no longer with us.

However, since the time the carousel opened to the public (1911, by the way), there have been dedicated employees—carpenters, painters, electricians, and artists—who have maintained the look and interworking's of this incredible machine. Because of their continued work and dedication, many more generations of families will be able to enjoy it.

In fact, many employees have come and gone between the time it opened and the time this book was written. I don't know many exactly, but it's been 106 years, so I'll let you do the generational math.

What does any of this have to do with leadership development? Good question.

To me, the people who built the carousel are like the people who recruit and hire our employees. (We can use new frontline employees OR leadership candidates as an example here—it works the same for both). Both are dealing with a finite process. You hire someone, or step them up to a leadership role, and the process is done. Just like the building of a carousel is a finite process, with a definite beginning and ending.

The people who got the carousel up and running, tweaking the operation until it was just perfect, are like the trainers, or initial training processes that a frontline employee or a new leader will experience. For frontline folks, this could be orientation or divisional training. For a new leader, this could be going through any leadership development opportunities offered by your company. Again, it's a finite process. You go to training and are then sent out on the job.

And then there are the folks who, for 106 years, have been carefully maintaining, painting, fixing, and running the carousel. To me, these are like the established leaders, with whom new leaders and frontline employees interact with daily—the ones who do their schedule, develop their skills, back them up when they make a mistake, encourage them when they are on the right track, etc. Just by sheer time, these folks play a HUGE role in the development, training, and performance of their teams, just like those folks who have been taking care of the carousel for 106 years. This is by no means a finite process ... it goes on as long as the employee is employed.

With that perspective, let's compare the potential influence of each process to the overall performance of a new leader.

On a 10-point scale, with 10 being the top,
here is what this information tells us:

Process	Score	Description
Recruiting/ Hiring	4	This is an important, foundational process. Without the right people in the right places, everything else gets more difficult. Patrick is (unfortunately) a great example of that. Because this is a finite process, the influence on the overall, long-term performance is low.
Training/ Onboard-ing	4	This is the start of the "orientation" process; getting people acclimated to their new role. New skills are learned, old habits are broken and new habits are formed. Again, this is a finite process, so its influence over long-term performance is low.
Support/ Long–term Develop-ment	9	As we saw in the carousel example, this phase is the longest, and therefore is the most influential. There are many more points of contact that can influence an individual's work habits. Because this phase essentially lasts for the remainder of the employee's tenure, it rates very high in terms of overall influence. It does not rate a 10 because it can't exist alone.

Here is what I find really interesting about these findings. In my experience, when a new employee or leader is not performing, doesn't behave, doesn't show up, is rude to guests, doesn't get along with team members, etc., the first thing managers tend to blame is the hiring.

"We just don't have any good candidates."

"People don't want or need to work like they used to."

"Everyone else is paying more and we can't compete."

They spend time and money revamping their hiring process with small overall results. Why? Because hiring wasn't the problem.

"Well, it must be the training, then. We've got to beef up the orientation process."

Okay, we can throw some dollars and resources at that, but …

Yep, you guessed it—minimal overall improvements.

What I almost never hear people say is that it's the management … that it's how employees are treated once they are out in the field … that the fact that they are now spending a significant amount of their waking and working hours in an environment where there is no one saying thank you, they don't provide tools or access to the information you need, and they yell at you if you mess up. Why can no one see that THIS—not hiring, not training—is the true culprit for employees leaving or underperforming? Again, this goes for frontline employees, as well as new leaders.

It truly boggles my mind when I hear an operational manager talk about improving hiring and training practices when the employee worked for them for three months. Do you honestly think that those two processes, which took up two to four days of the employee's life could really hold a candle to the influence you have had over that employee for the last three months? Four days versus three months—I'm no math major, but I think I see where this is going.

On the other hand, my mind is not so boggled ... I addressed this in the *Myth of Employee Burnout*, but it bears repeating here. If you can't see (or admit) that you are part of the problem, you can't see that you are also part of the solution. If people are leaving, not providing service, or not developing leadership skills, that absolutely falls most squarely on management's shoulders—not on hiring or training. To me this epiphany sheds additional light on where the true influence lies.

Chapter 13
Patrick and the Terrible, Horrible, No Good, Very Bad Promotion (Selection)

Let's think back to Patrick, the outstanding service provider that we thought would make a great team leader. As we learned, there is a lot more to selecting a leader than just bestowing a title upon someone and getting them a new name tag.

As we mentioned earlier in the book, it's possible that Patrick felt pressured into taking on a leadership role. If you are choosing new leaders, your first question to each of them should be: How do you feel about taking on a leadership role?

There are many ways to find this out. If you hold interviews for leadership positions, this is certainly a question I would ask. And yes, you should conduct interviews for leadership positions.

Before we talk about interviews, let's take a step back. If you agree that these leadership roles you are filling are important to your business, then it's critical that you put the time, effort, and energy into finding the right people for these jobs. Yes, it will take longer. Yes, it will take more scrutiny. But think about the pickles you have likely been in in the past due to poor leadership. Think about the times you have had to replace someone (or really WANTED to replace them, but didn't or couldn't).

For many, the interview is the first (and maybe only) step in the assessment process. This is management's one and only chance to see what this person will bring to the table. If experience is any guide, this is not enough information—especially for leadership positions.

Do your employees fill out an application for employment? Then it stands to reason that your leaders should fill out an application to be in a leadership position. If you already do this, great! If not, here are some things you can find out about a leadership candidate if they have to fill out and turn in an application:

▶ **You know who is interested in the position** – Assuming the application process is voluntary, only people who are interested in the positions will take the time to fill them out. The best part about this is that you may have some hidden leadership talent lurking in the shadows, and you would never know it, if you only looked to promote the outgoing kids with the big personalities.

▶ **You will see who can follow directions** – In addition to the questions you may ask, it's also telling when you include very specific instructions to see if applicants are reading and paying attention. If being submitted with pen and paper, ask them to use a certain color pen, or indicate that a particular page is to be left blank ... anything to break up the process and see if they are paying attention.

▶ **You can get an idea of how they think** – You can also get this from the interview, but the application gives people an opportunity to express their thoughts in a different medium. Since the written (or typed) word is still something leaders use to communicate, you need to see how well they can use that skill. Can they put together cohesive thoughts and get their point across?

▶ **You can get a sense of their creativity and problem solving** – One leadership application I saw was simply a blank piece of paper. They handed it to the applicants and said turn it in by a certain date. Some people drew pictures, some quoted authors, and others wrote about their leadership experience. It allowed them to show their personality in a creative way. You can also have applicants make a video or use some other creative medium to share their personality. One company said, only submit a video, and they discarded any paper resumes and applications, because the candidates hadn't followed directions.

With the applications in play, now we really have something to talk about in the interview. No matter what method you used, now is the time to follow up on what they said on the application and dig into their interpretation of what it means to be a leader. And, of course, to see if it gels with what you are looking for.

And what are you looking for? Sometimes it's difficult to quantify what you are seeking in a leader, but that's exactly what you have to do, if you are going to pick ones that will ultimately help you run your business.

Do you need someone who will be a role model? How about someone who understands the business vision and goals, and is willing to hold others accountable to them? I'll bet you would like someone who can make decisions, solve problems, and think on their feet. Oh, and what about someone who can rally troops, keeping the team working together? Is this a good start?

If we start with a basic interview, of course, you can ask behavioral questions to get people to share examples of the desired actions. If you are not familiar with behavioral interviewing questions, they are simply statements or inquiries that ask about specific situations that a person has been in. The goal is for the candidate to be able to relay exact actions that they took to solve a problem or satisfy a guest or team member request/need. The basis for this technique is that generally speaking, previous behaviors are the best indication of future behaviors.

Here are some examples of leadership behavioral questions that could be included in an interview:

▶ Tell me about a time when you had to resolve a conflict between two people. What was the situation and how did you handle it?

▶ Describe a situation where you strongly disagreed with a coworker but it was important to maintain a

163

professional relationship. What happened and how did you deal with it?

▶ Tell me about your worst guest complaint. What was the complaint and how did you satisfy the guest?

This is also a time when you will want to assess future decision making ability by presenting some scenarios to work through. Anything you can do to simulate the situations and conditions they will face once in the role, the better idea you will have about their ability to handle it.

Here are a few samples of scenarios that you could have a candidate talk through:

▶ You have two employees that want the same day off, but only one of them can have it. What do you do?

▶ One of your best employees just had a guest complaint against them. The guest accused them of being rude and giving the wrong change. How do you handle this?

▶ You are a supervisor in the rides department. As you are walking along the midway, you notice a trash can that is overflowing. Just then you get a call on the radio that a ride across the park has e-stopped. On the way to the ride, you notice a child has dropped his ice cream cone and is crying. What do you do?

From this you will see how they think through problems and what sort of analytical tools they already have in their tool belt.

Taking the interview process a step further, David

Crandall, General Manager of Fiesta Village Fun Park in California (fiestavillage.com), also requires leadership candidates to create and deliver a ten to fifteen-minute presentation to the current leadership team about their leadership philosophies and what kind of leader they would be.

David said he was blown away by the creativity and passion that the applicants showed. Being able to express themselves in that way really brought out many of the leadership qualities David hoped they possessed. And now he didn't have to guess.

Application and interview processes are great ways to get a sense if you have a true leadership candidate in front of you, or if they are better suited to not suit up as a supervisor.

To get an even better idea of who they are and how they will perform in the role, let's take a few steps even further back.

Let's go back to before you needed to hire these leaders. Maybe a few weeks or months. If you run a seasonal operation, maybe even stepping back to the previous season.

Since it's a leader's job to look ahead and make a plan for their operation, why should the process of selecting new leaders be any different? Why not start planning for your next year's leadership team now?

A few chapters ago, we met a young overachiever named Mikaela. We didn't have an official leadership spot available, but started considering other responsibilities to allow Mikaela to take on.

Remember this list?

- ▶ Cleaning crews
- ▶ Daily or weekly meetings
- ▶ Staff parties
- ▶ Organizing or updating training materials
- ▶ Performing the training itself

These were some things (and it's not an exhaustive list) that we thought Mikaela could take over. These would give her a little more responsibility while also keeping her engaged in the job.

And, oh, by the way … did we mention that this also gives YOU the chance to observe how Mikaela would handle the extra responsibility? Yeah. Big bonus there.

This is what I mean by stepping way back to start the leadership "interview" process. If you are looking for leaders in 2018, start in 2017.

Giving Mikaela extra jobs, projects, and tasks that she can perform and you can evaluate her on, gives you that much more data to go on when choosing someone to be in a leadership role. Wouldn't you like to know in July of 2017 that Mikaela is not the leader you thought she would be, rather than finding out after you officially promoted her in 2018?

That said, what if you get into 2018 and one of your newly promoted leaders is struggling? They aced the interview, did an unbelievable presentation, and excelled at the extra tasks last season. But now, in the throes of a real leadership position, they aren't working out. What do you do?

Yes, you will coach them and give them a chance to improve. But if improvement doesn't happen (even incremental improvement), if they are not performing up to your standards, then it's time to talk about other options. They probably (hopefully) haven't done anything egregious enough to get fired, but you know you can't keep them in a leadership role any longer.

The longer they stay in an active, influential role, the greater the potential damage to the team, themselves, and the company. That's the opposite of what you want from a leader ... you need someone you can trust, who will carry out the company mission, and do their best to serve the needs of the employees in their charge.

Which is why you need a process ... a procedure ... a course of action to take when this happens. Notice I said *when*, not *if*. We are dealing with human beings here, not robots. You cannot predict with 100% accuracy what someone is going to do or how they will handle themselves when the curtain goes up. As thorough as we can be, someone will slip through the cracks.

So we need to be ready. Before you hire your next leader, think about the scenarios that would end a supervisor's tenure. Make a list. Rate the offences by severity, just like you would for a frontline employee. What would constitute actions such as immediate termination, a coaching, a reassignment within the department, or reassignment outside the department? Once you have that list, make sure that all the leaders within your company are on board, and will hold their supervisors to the same standards.

Next, discuss what will happen if you do need to make a change. Will the person revert to frontline pay if they stay in the company? What does that conversation sound like? When does it happen? Where does it happen? Who conducts the conversation? What happens directly after the conversation takes place?

One angle we haven't considered yet is: what if the supervisor decides the position isn't for them? That has to be worked into the process as well, and communicated up front.

In the spirit of fairness and transparency for the new leader, they need to know about this process. Best to talk about this before they accept the position, so they have a clear picture of what they are walking into. However, the chance of termination or demotion should not be used as a fear tactic or "motivator" to keep people on the right track. Not even close.

It should be explained that as their supervisor, you have an obligation to continue to evaluate their performance, and you will do everything you can to ensure they are successful. You will provide resources, tools, and guidance on a regular basis, and invite questions and feedback about their experience. Should performance dip below an acceptable level, measures will be taken to help the new leader improve. If the trend continues without signs of getting better, conversations will be held about whether this is the right position or not.

Like everything else in the world of leadership this is a balancing act. How do you know when to pull the plug? How do you know when enough is enough?

In this case, it's probably best to err on the side of caution. Matt Ouimet, CEO of Cedar Fair, once said that early in his career, one of his biggest management mistakes was keeping ineffective leaders in position for too long. Think of the damage a reluctant leader will have ... morale, productivity, efficiency, team dynamics, guest service ... I could go on. When a person is losing trust and respect from their team, it's like driving down an icy road—there isn't much you can do but hang on and hope you land softly in a snow bank.

As a leader of leaders though, you do have options. If you have established at the beginning of the relationship that changes will be made if performance slips, you have an out. You have the opportunity, as well as the responsibility, to do something about it.

All of this is well and good IF you have the leadership positions to promote someone to AND if they actually want to be a leader. It's not a very productive practice to promote someone to a leadership role just because you don't know what else to do with them (and their talents).

What if you have more applicants than positions? When my friend David Crandall started asking leadership applicants to come up with a presentation, he actually ended up getting more and more people wanting to be involved. He said that one year, he had seven supremely qualified people (and he knew they were qualified by his pre-screening and their presentations) and only five spots to fill. Know what he did? He created two more supervisor spots. Kind of the opposite way to think about it ... so often we are cutting staff and trying to be more efficient. David found that by adding these extra supervisors, each supervisor had fewer people to oversee, which actually DID make them more efficient.

I recognize that adding more supervisor positions isn't always possible or even within your control, but it is something to think about if you have more people than current positions.

This is where you could apply some creativity to figure out how to tap into their talents and passions WITHOUT promoting them to a leadership position.

What are their talents? Maybe a lateral move is more in order. Maybe they are in the games department, but will be studying criminal justice. What about a transfer to security? What if they are great with graphic design, but were hired as a cook? Does marketing have any openings? Maybe even the internal communication (newsletters, employee portals, employee blog) could use as a refresher.

These positions don't even have to be permanent ... even temporary assignments allow them to use their talents until something else opens up. Know your people and be creative. Even ask them. Don't think you have to come up with this stuff all on your own.

The other scenario is if they don't want to be a leader. Sometimes people need a little encouragement if they don't think they are ready, and that is fine. Letting them know what the position is all about and that you will be there to support this is great, and if that tips the scale, sweet. If they are more adamant, like Patrick, let it go. The last thing you need is a reluctant leader on your hands.

Chapter 14
Here Are Your Keys and Your Radio – GO! (Training)

And so it happens, you have a group of newly promoted leaders standing in front of you at the beginning of the season. They will never be more ready than at this moment to take in your words of wisdom, to hear and absorb your stories of the ebb and flow of leadership and to fill their minds with the positive possibilities and opportunities of being a leader.

And you say, "Make sure your paperwork is in on time."

Oh, the horror.

I do understand why we spend so much time on paperwork, forms, and admin processes with our new leaders—because that's what could land us in hot water down the road. If there is an incident, a savvy lawyer will ask for your log sheets, witness statements, and training documentation to see if all the i's are dotted and t's are crossed. If they aren't, you'll be in for a world of hurt.

So, make sure your paperwork is not only turned in on time, but is also filled out correctly.

Again, I get it.

What I also get is that leaders typically don't fail because of paperwork. It's usually because of an inability to lead their staff, not being a productive part of the leadership team, or being such a reluctant leader that nothing, and I mean nothing, gets done.

So in addition to the paperwork training, we also have to train them to be a leader. Yes, we've gone through the process of selecting people with some natural leadership ability, but that doesn't mean that they will take on the qualities of a perfect leader right out of the gate. They still need guidance, they still need information, and they still need tools to be able to do their jobs.

In March of 2017, I was lucky enough to do a webinar for the IAAPA (International Association of Amusement Parks and Attractions). On that webinar, I asked the participants about their challenges with training new supervisors. Here is what they said:

- ▶ 68% - not enough time
- ▶ 18% - don't know what material to train them on
- ▶ 14% - don't know how to train another leader

Since many places DO train on paperwork and admin, that must mean that the *time* they are talking about has to do with soft skills. Teaching leaders how to coach, to resolve conflict, to build rapport, to manage their time, to delegate, to create a team atmosphere, to listen, to follow-up on commitments, and to be a positive role model … just to name a few of the things leaders REALLY need to do to be successful.

But due to the seasonality of many businesses and the availability of people typically put into leadership roles, time is of the essence. You may only have time to get them up to speed on the paperwork, maybe provide some level of soft skills awareness training, and then send them off to battle.

"That's the way I learned, that's the way you learned, and darn it, that's the way these new leaders will learn." (stomps foot)

If those numbers tell us anything though, there is a desire to teach other things, but the time and knowhow might not be there. So how do you train someone on all of those things, given the challenges and limitations of the real world?

First, you must realize that you WILL NOT be able to train everyone on everything all at once. It's impossible. It's a nice thought to be able to give your new leaders all the skills and information they need right at the beginning of the season or their tenure, but it's not practical from time standpoint, nor is it effective from a learning perspective.

It takes time to learn a new skill or process, and learning the ins and outs of leadership is no exception. When thinking about this a few years ago, my mind made an interesting connection between the training and development of people versus developing a picture. Probably because they both used the word "develop," but I digress ...

In the not too distant past, everyone who took a picture had to open up their camera, remove a stock of film and take it to a special location to have it "developed." Even in my lifetime, that process went from about a week, to a day, to an hour. This was how you got your pictures printed so that you could put them in a scrapbook, photo album, or shoe box for safekeeping. During this process, you didn't know if you had a good picture or a bad picture, or if it was blurry or your heads were cut off. You just didn't know … so you waited.

Now, pictures are "developed" (or available for viewing) instantly. Within a nanosecond, you can see if your selfie, groupie, or image of your decadent dessert is good enough to share or has to be taken again. The technology has brought us instant feedback on our photographic pursuits.

The other side of that relationship is about how people develop. It's not nearly that fast.

Because technology has surged ahead, and we can do so many more things at a blistering rate, I think that has caused many people to think that the human brain is able to develop that much faster, too. If we can see in a nanosecond what used to take a week, then the human brain should be able to process in a nanosecond what used to take a week.

But it doesn't work that way. Not even close.

If it did, we'd be driving at age 8. Graduating high school at age 10. Voting at age 12.

But we don't. Our minds have not caught up with technology. Or I should say the speed at which we develop our thought processes and judgments have not caught up with the speed it takes to develop a picture. In fact, the way our mind learns, develops, cognates, and processes critical information has not changed in literally thousands of years. And it's likely that it won't change in a thousand more.

So, that means that if we want to develop these soft skills, if we want leaders to be able to process information and make sound, valuable judgments, we must invest the time. There is just no other answer. There is no short cut. There is no app. It's a non-negotiable.

What is negotiable, however, is *when* we spend the time. Remember when we talked about planning your leadership team the year before you needed them? During that time, you can be building communication and time management skills. You can help them develop critical thinking so they can make effective decisions. And all the while you can be observing them, coaching them, and guiding them.

Let's say that you assigned Mikaela, your star leadership candidate for next season, to run a morning cleaning crew. She was responsible for getting the staff she needed, rounding up the supplies, coordinating with maintenance to make sure the area to be cleaned was ready—but not during morning safety checks—and documenting the hours worked for the payroll department. You met with her a week before the cleaning crew was scheduled and went over all this information, even giving it to her on a checklist.

This brought up several questions from Mikaela:

▶ Who does she coordinate with in maintenance?

▶ Where does she get the supplies?

▶ How does she give the hours worked information to payroll?

All good questions, right? And good that they are being asked before the morning of the cleaning crew! She gets the information and is on her way.

After the cleaning crew session takes place, you now follow up with Mikaela, maybe later that day or the following day (don't wait too long). You ask her how it went, did she have everything she needed, how did the employees do, and did she have any trouble getting the information to payroll?

Then the question you should ask that will get her thinking like a leader is: *What could be improved for next time?*

Now she is thinking ... well, if we had just one more person, we could have covered even more area. If we had more time, we could have done a deeper cleaning. If I would have taken the time to organize the crews better, maybe with a checklist of what was to be cleaned, they wouldn't have had to come back to me every time they finished one task, or they wouldn't just be sitting around waiting for me to assign them with another area to clean.

So ... next time, what will Mikaela do? "I'll come up with a checklist for the crew to keep them on track and maximize the amount of time we have to spend."

Excellent. Mikaela is now thinking more like a leader. These are the types of experiences that "train" people to behave like a leader should behave. And the best part is, Mikaela isn't even in an official leadership role yet.

In addition to the "what" could have been improved, it's also critical to talk about "why" things maybe didn't go according to plan or why a different approach would have gotten a different (possibly better) result. People (and leaders *are* people) rarely change what they do without understanding the reasons "why" behind it.

Now what if Mikaela totally failed on the cleaning crew? What if she didn't contact the people she was supposed to, didn't get the supplies, and nothing got cleaned? Did Mikaela fail? Partially, but so did we. Maybe we didn't recognize that Mikaela wasn't ready for this. Maybe when we went over the checklist, we did it too fast and didn't give Mikaela the chance to ask any questions. Maybe the directions we gave were unclear. Maybe, maybe, maybe.

Or maybe we were as clear as could be and Mikaela did ask her clarifying questions. Maybe Mikaela just didn't have the get-up-and-go to get this done. Again, better to know this the season *before* than to put Mikaela in a position, give her the keys and radio and THEN realize that she wasn't right for the job.

Remember, in this scenario, we are working a season ahead. This experience with Mikaela was happening the season before we were considering her for an official leadership position. If it worked out, your training has already begun. If it didn't, the search for your next leader will continue.

If you operate year-round, don't let the "seasonal" talk get in the way of the concept. You have an even greater opportunity to spend the time with people before they need to step into an official leadership role.

To me, this proves the point that we should be training early, and training often. Find as many of those opportunities as you can that allow you to assess someone's leadership acumen while also training them on the critical soft skills of being a leader.

Does this mean this all must fall to you? No! This is a tremendous opportunity to further develop your current leadership team. Get your (seasonal) supervisor to lead Mikaela through the cleaning crew process, follow up with her, and evaluate her progress. Then you do the same with your supervisor.

Ultimately, you are now teaching a thought process, a mindset. We already talked about the Leadership mindset earlier in the book. This will be the critical change that allows people to switch, in their minds, from frontline mentality to leadership mentality so they can make the decisions and judgment calls that are necessary at the leadership level. It just takes time.

My friend Aaron Corr at TreeUmph Adventure Course

(treeumph.com) shared with me their philosophy on developing leaders within their company. The following tips are some excerpts of how TreeUmph encourages their guides to think, and ultimately act, like leaders.

Tips for Guides Wanting to Be Managers

Leadership qualities that are important at TreeUmph: thinking like an owner, not like a manager or an employee. This includes:

- ✓ Being willing to consider what a guest, fellow staff member or manager may be thinking, feeling, and wanting and then going above and beyond to help them.
- ✓ Creating TEAM by contributing and helping responsibly while allowing everyone else to do the same.
- ✓ Letting go of what makes you look good or feel powerful and help others look good and feel powerful.
- ✓ Taking the high road, always.
- ✓ Understanding that when someone is upset with you that they probably have a very different perspective on the situation than you do and that communicating about it is the only way to resolve it.
- ✓ Providing exemplary guest service, actually listening to what the guest is saying, understanding their complaint or concern and going out of your way to help because you WANT to help them. Do all this without sacrificing safety or efficiency. A different perspective is the key to being effective—the guests felt they deserved what they

got or what they were asking for, even if you didn't. Don't ever talk about how lame the guest is for asking for the service, whether they are standing in front of you or they have left the park.

✓ Be able to think and respond quickly and decisively on your feet based on the needs of the park and with safety foremost in your mind. Don't be afraid of making a wrong decision and looking bad.

✓ Understand that every guest (current and potential) is of utmost importance. How they feel about their experience and what they tell people IS who we are. It is all we are.

✓ Understand that every guide is of utmost importance. How they feel about their experience and what they tell people IS who we are. It is all we are.

✓ Give up thinking you know what leadership is, there are always improvements that can be made—be confident, but be humble and flexible in your approach.

✓ Never be afraid to ask, anyone, anything. Everyone you work with has value and may be able to help solve a problem in a way that you can learn from.

✓ Never stop trying to communicate effectively with everyone.

✓ Encourage fun—be the fun ringleader sometimes, but allow others to take that role,   too.

✓ Always consider your presentation—not to your friends and fellow guides, but to   our guests. You can manufacture your presentation to them. Your presentation to your friends and fellow guides is beyond your consideration.

181

It will be only who you are, day in and day out.

✓ You are already a leader, so look for what can improve the TEAM, the park, and the experience for everyone.

✓ The most valuable leaders at TreeUmph are those that can build new leaders.

That last one to me is critical. Leaders lead others to be productive, yes. But they are also responsible for developing other leaders along the way. How can leaders build up other leaders if they weren't given the time and tools to develop themselves? No matter how you were trained or taught as a leader, you also have the responsibility to build up and develop other leaders, not just task managers.

The folks at Fiesta Village Family Fun Park also have put together an amazing resource for new leaders. Every year they have their leadership team document all the different situations and scenarios they go through and all of the lessons they have learned. That information goes into a document that is given to new Supervisors so they can get an idea early on of the vast and varied types of things they will be asked to deal with. It goes beyond the S.O.P. because it covers much more of the gray areas a leader typically has to deal with.

Chapter 15
Learning Doesn't Stop When You Stop Training (Support)

We've already established that training, especially for new leaders, is not a one-time proposition. Training early and often means you might be starting to build leadership skills before they ever get into the position, but it also means the continued training is just that … continued. And often.

One of the first things we should do in pursuit of supporting our new leaders is to let them know we are doing it. Sit down with them and explain that your job is to help them be successful. What will that process look like? What can they expect? No one gets better by doing the same things they have always done, so prepare your new leaders to get thrust into situations that will remove them from their comfort zone. Set an expectation that you will be providing feedback on their performance and that you will also expect feedback from them.

You are also there to Involve, Encourage, Develop, and Guide them, just like we discussed that they will be doing for their employees. Just because it's in the book doesn't mean they will embrace it without question. You will have to teach them and make sure they learn and apply those concepts.

Problem is, we don't truly learn how to do something from just one experience, do we? Especially when it comes to leadership concepts, it takes repeated exposure to the ideas before they truly sink in. Having Mikaela run a cleaning crew once will not allow her to finely hone those skills. So that means new leaders not only have to be selected and initially trained properly, but we have to continue to support their development as long as they are leaders. That's how you build the leaders you are supposed to be building.

Remember that we can't get everyone to learn everything all at the same time, so we start with the basics and build from there. The basics could include communication skills (including listening), coaching, and time management. As a leader gets more comfortable, we can work in things like delegation, problem solving, and conflict resolution.

When do we work these in, you ask? We're very busy once the season gets rolling!

Yes, you are, but I would bet that there is a time, maybe weekly, when you are already getting together with your leadership staff to go over recent happenings, incidents and policy changes. I'll bet, if you really tried, you could set aside 10-15% of that meeting time to professional development. I'm not talking about trying to cover a college ethics course in fifteen-minute increments, but you could watch a Ted Talk and then discuss. You could have everyone read an article or listen to a podcast and talk about what they took away from it.

How about using the book club model? Get a book for everyone on a relevant topic, then talk about a chapter or section at each meeting.

You could introduce the topic of delegation, give them a tool, and challenge them to use it the following week. Then the next meeting rolls around and you spend a few minutes talking about how it went. Who delegated something? How did it go? What could have gone better? What did you learn? An aside—probably the least productive thing you can do is ask someone to read, watch, or do something and then NOT follow up on it. What's the point? That's certainly what your employees will be asking.

"She wanted us to read this article,
but then we never did anything with it."

What are the chances they will read the next article you ask them to? Yep, slim to none.

There, in fifteen minutes you started the ball rolling for some leadership skills development. Didn't that feel good? And now you know that you can do it every week! Is time such a big issue now?

If you want to get really ambitious, set aside a special time for development, away from your meeting. If you make it a priority and it delivers value, your team will see the value and make it priority, too.

Another way to formalize this ongoing learning is through a mentorship program. This allows the new leaders to get input and perspective from a trusted and experienced leader

185

who isn't their direct supervisor. This is important. Later in this chapter we will discuss one-on-one meetings that leaders can (and should) have with the people on their teams.

Mentorship

A mentor/mentee relationship is designed to be different than that of a boss and subordinate, in that a mentor provides guidance and suggestions—not work direction. A mentor is also a teacher, a listener, and advisor … someone who can connect the dots and find the leadership lessons in everyday occurrences.

Here are some key things to think about when setting up a mentorship program at your facility:

▶ **Develop criteria for matching mentors with mentees.** This is an important relationship, so there should be some reason that a mentor and mentee are paired together. For example: does the mentor hold a position or have experience with something the mentee hopes to achieve? Is the mentor someone the potential mentee knows from previous work and is someone they respect and admire?

▶ **Do not force anyone to be a mentor.** While the skills needed to be a mentor are important leadership skills, that doesn't mean that everyone in a leadership role has the "right stuff" to be a mentor. Like new leaders, a reluctant mentor will be ineffective at best, destructive at worst.

▶ **Define mentor/mentee relationship.** Because there is no reporting structure in place, there needs to be a mentor/mentee structure set up:

When will you meet and how often?

- Weekly or biweekly for 30-60 minutes is a good starting point

How many meetings will there be?

- Will this last all season or until a specific point?

What are appropriate topics of discussion?

- Anything impacting working environment
- Set up parameters if discussions indicate abuse or illegal activity

What do participants (both mentors and mentees) need/want out of the relationship to make it successful?

What happens if a meeting is missed?

What's the best method of communication between meetings?

What is each person expected to bring or prepare for each meeting?

▶ **Mentor** – listening ear, open mind, ability to identify behavioral trends, and leadership lessons, no judgment

▶ **Mentee** – open mind, current situations and examples of how they were handled, questions, thoughts, opinions

187

▶ **Meetings don't need to be overly structured or scheduled**—just a chance to talk and explore what's been going on, which can happen in many places— the park, in an office, or over lunch

▶ **Reinforce the importance of the process.** Mentors should let their mentees know how seriously they are taking the process by showing up to meetings on time, leading effective conversations, and acknowledging progress. Effective conversations may include only one question and then active listening … if that's what's appropriate for that meeting, so be it. Mentoring is not about forcing an agenda, so much as it is about supporting individuals' development at their own pace.

One of the great benefits of establishing an effective mentorship program is that you prepare more and more of your leaders to become mentors in the future.

For example, let's say you are a fulltime manager who is mentoring a seasonal lead. That lead comes back the following season as a supervisor, and they are mentored again by another manager. The third season they come back again as a supervisor, and now potentially have the experience to mentor an up-and-coming lead. What a great development opportunity for them as well!

Eventually, you get more people who CAN mentor, so you get more people who ARE mentored. It's a beautiful way to keep the leadership pipeline full of promising talent.

As this example illustrates, this is not an overnight process. Like anything, it's best to start small, maybe in just a few departments, and see how it goes. Collect lots of feedback from that first year and use it to strengthen the program going forward.

So whether it's formal or informal training tactics, what topics or concepts should we be covering to support new leaders in their role?

For insight on that, I thought it would be good to share some data that I got from the attendees at the World Waterpark Association's Annual Symposium & Trade Show in 2016. I asked them about their #1 challenge with new supervisors. See if any of these rings true for you:

#1 Challenge with new supervisors

- ✓ You're their leader—not their friend
- ✓ Understand their role
- ✓ They're now in charge
- ✓ Form good working relationship between supervisors and managers
- ✓ Don't lose qualities that got you promoted
- ✓ Practice what you preach
- ✓ Model expected behavior
- ✓ Make them understand "leader" isn't a title

If we go back to our section on training, how many of these things have to do with paperwork? None. They all have to do with interpersonal relationships and accepting and embracing the role and mindset of a leader.

What this tells me is that not enough time has been spent on these topics while developing new leaders. Perhaps these were people who did a great job teaching policy, but fell short with how to build relationships and be a positive influence. I would bet dollars to donuts these are the same people who say they don't have enough time to train their leaders.

We've already seen that there are different times to train leaders than just at the beginning of the season or when they take the role. We now need to shift our thinking to realize that every day is a learning opportunity. That each encounter and every experience can yield a teaching moment that can help build skills in new leaders. We just have to see those for what they are and act accordingly.

One of the first things we can do is always have in our minds to "follow up" with new leaders. This could be after a training class, when a project is completed, after an incident in the park, or an encounter with a guest. Here's how this might go.

Fast forward to 2018 and our leadership superstar, Mikaela, has been promoted to a lead in the Admissions area. She deals with a lot of guests, which means she also deals with complaints. One day, you get the call to go up to Guest Services to assist with a guest. Mikaela has been trying to resolve the issue, but it's not going well.

When you get there, you realize that Mikaela has said and done what you consider right, but it hasn't been working. You step in, listen to the guest, and say pretty much the same things Mikaela has been saying. This time, the guest calms down and accepts your explanation. What just happened?

Since you have been doing this a long time, you know that sometimes a guest just needs to hear the explanation from someone else—usually a person in a higher position of authority—before they will believe it. There is also the psychological phenomenon of not wanting to lose face with the person you originally got into an altercation with. So, the guest holds their ground with Mikaela but gives in almost immediately to her manager. I've seen this too many times to count.

The point is that you know what just happened, but Mikaela doesn't. She doesn't have the experience you do, and without some additional discussion, she may start to feel that she did something wrong, that there was another tactic to try, or that the guest just had a problem with her gender or skin color.

This is where you need to follow up and explain what just happened. Take a few minutes and see what Mikaela thought of the situation, then share your experience and perspective. This will help Mikaela understand what really happened, so she doesn't judge the situation too harshly.

Now this isn't just a guest complaint, it's a leadership development teaching moment.

How about if there is an incident? Maybe a ride evacuation or a fire in the kitchen? It's one thing to address the issue in the moment, it's quite another to follow up with the leadership team to find out what may have caused the situation and what can be done better in the future.

And maybe it's nothing … maybe the situation was an anomaly that would have taken a miracle to prevent. Then what about how you handled it? Were the guests taken care of? Were all the employees safe? What steps could be taken in the future to be even more efficient, careful, or proactive in these situations?

If you have a plan to deal with emergencies, and you practiced that plan, was the plan carried out in a real situation? Were all the steps followed?

That's stuff that leaders think about. Never too early to get newly promoted leaders thinking in that same direction, too.

In any of these cases, don't be afraid to ask this question, "What did you learn?" Sometimes it is obvious, other times it's not. Sometimes we don't really realize we actually learned something until someone points it out to us. Once that happens, though, it goes into our memory banks as new, important data or information, and we are more likely to be able to recall it easily in the future.

In Part I of this book, we talked a lot about trust and how important that is for a new leader to establish with their team. There is another side to that coin as we talk about how management supports the development of the leaders in their charge.

And in this context, it's about how establishing trust can allow people the latitude to take chances and do the things they think are right. Here's an example.

When I was an Operations Area Manager at Valleyfair, I oversaw Park Services, Admissions, and Challenge Park. I was very lucky to inherit some great seasonal supervisors in each department, including Lisa in Admissions. Lisa had worked at the park for ten years already when I got there, and I was sure she had already forgotten more than I was going to be able to learn. She was an incredible asset and I counted on her to show me the ropes.

Something happened during my first season at that park that I honestly had not anticipated—especially with Lisa. She was well-versed in all park policies and has probably seen just about every situation, yet she would seek my opinion and approval when dealing with certain guest situations. Granted, they were "elevated" situations, but still, I figured she had dealt with worse in the past.

And then it hit me. She didn't trust me yet. Or more specifically, she didn't trust that she could make a big-time decision and that I would be okay with it. We hadn't established that relationship or level of trust yet. So, in order to do that, I started redirecting the question back to her.

When she would ask me about a situation, I would ask her, "What do you think we should do?" 9.5 times out of 10, it was exactly what I thought we should do, too. The other .5 time, we just made a minor tweak to her proposed solution and went with it. I think these exchanges helped build the trust between Lisa and me, because it showed that we were on the same page. And for Lisa, it defined the parameters within which she could make decisions on her own, versus having to run the idea by someone else.

How often do we get the input of our employees in those situations? We likely are in problem-solving mode, so we prescribe a course of action and expect our employees to implement it. By getting their input, we not only get a glimpse into their thought process, but we also allow them to put their own solutions into action. That's confidence-building and support at its best!

Another way to keep the communication open between you and your new leader is by having regular one-on-one meetings. These can happen in an office, in the park, at a coffee shop … the important thing is that they happen consistently and that there is an agenda and/or objective to the time you are spending together.

For example, if you set aside 30 minutes for a one-on-one, here is a sample agenda to follow for that time.

- 0 – 10 minutes – What's going on with you?
- 10 – 20 minutes – What's going on with the team?
- 20 – 30 minutes – How can I help?

This basic framework gives a reason for the meeting, but also allows you to focus on what's important. You may not get past the first question in some meetings, and that's okay. The idea is that you have taken the time to meet and you are continually talking about *something*. The only way you will get the feedback and information that you need from your supervisors is if the lines of communication are open.

Depending on your initial relationship with the new supervisor, don't expect a lot of deep conversations right off the bat. This is as much about strengthening your relationship as it about sharing information. It may take some time for them to trust you enough to share, to see that you really are there to help, and to not be overwhelmed by the difference in organizational levels. Remember this new level of peer group is potentially opening up a whole new series of doubts and fears, and those will have to be dealt with before true sharing and communication can take place.

I mentioned that these meetings should happen consistently. I can't emphasize this enough. Miss just one meeting and it becomes way too easy to postpone or reschedule future meetings. This development opportunity should be a priority for you, and by you treating it that way, it will become a priority for your new leaders.

I call this a development opportunity as much as a meeting, because this is a chance for new leaders to ask questions, seek clarification, and to gain knowledge and guidance from you. You will probably learn things, too, if you keep your ears and your mind open.

As much as support means to continue to train and develop, it also has to mean being able to identify the need to take an alternate course.

In this way, we are coming full circle back to Patrick. He ended up quitting outright and that was a huge loss for the park. He still could have been a great operator, making lots of positive memories for thousands of families visiting over the summer. We let it get to a point where that was just not possible, but it didn't have to be that way. → *alternate option: lateral move, like I did*

During the selection process, we said it was a good idea to outline what would happen if either we, as the management team, or our new supervisor, decided that this just wasn't working out. This would be the time that you would enact that process.

Here's the good news, because you have decided to spend more time following up with and supporting your new supervisors, as well as having regular one-on-one meetings with them, you will either have the chance to guide them to success or spot the warning signs of a reluctant leader much sooner.

In addition, if you take the phrase "train early and train often" to heart, you will again be able to assess their skills *before* they get into the role, reducing the chance that you will be faced with this situation. It's not a guarantee, but you would rather play the better odds, wouldn't you?

Chapter 16
Enjoy the Ride

As a ride operator early in my career, I can't tell you how many times I must have uttered this phrase. And now, as we come to the end of the book, I would like to also offer you, the reader, a chance to "enjoy the ride."

In many ways, leadership is like a roller coaster, a tilt-a-whirl, a carousel and a Ferris wheel all at once. There are dips and curves, fast paced times, and slow. Sometimes you feel a little dizzy or unsettled and, at times, you are on top of the world and the view is amazing. It's not uncommon to lose track of which way you are going, as the sounds and stimuli around you wreak havoc with your sense of direction. And that's all on a good day.

Leadership is also not for the faint of heart. As tough as it is, as challenging as it can be, there should still be an element of *joy* you experience as you help and serve others. It feels good to do the right thing, and while it's not always easy, leaders have the opportunity to do right by their employees, peers, and companies every day. It's really more than an opportunity—it's a responsibility.

And the people who prepare the next generation of leaders have a responsibility, too—to train, nurture, guide, and ultimately prepare new leaders for their role. As this book has shown, it's so much more than selecting a person who happens to fit the suit.

It's also their job to identify when someone may fit the suit, but isn't wearing it well. There is no shame in either not wanting to be a leader or realizing that it's not for you once you get into it. You are not admitting defeat, you are learning important information about yourself. Not everyone likes the tilt-a-whirl, either. Whether you are leading for the first time, or you are leading other leaders, it's a rewarding journey that never really ends.

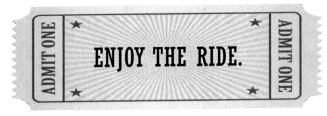

CPSIA information can be obtained
at www.ICGtesting.com
Printed in the USA
FFOW05n2310011117